MW01537840

THIS MUSIC NOTEBOOK BELONGS TO

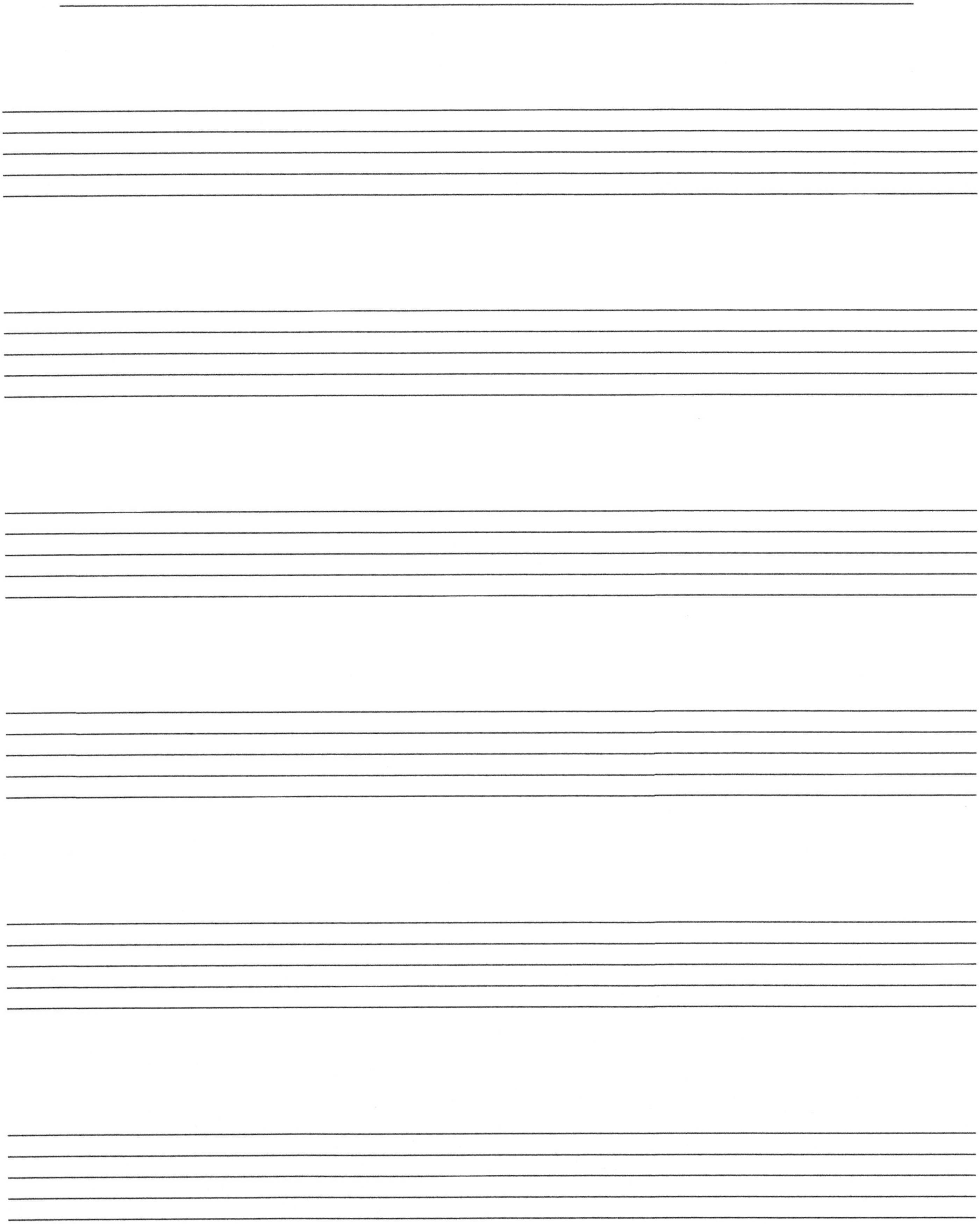

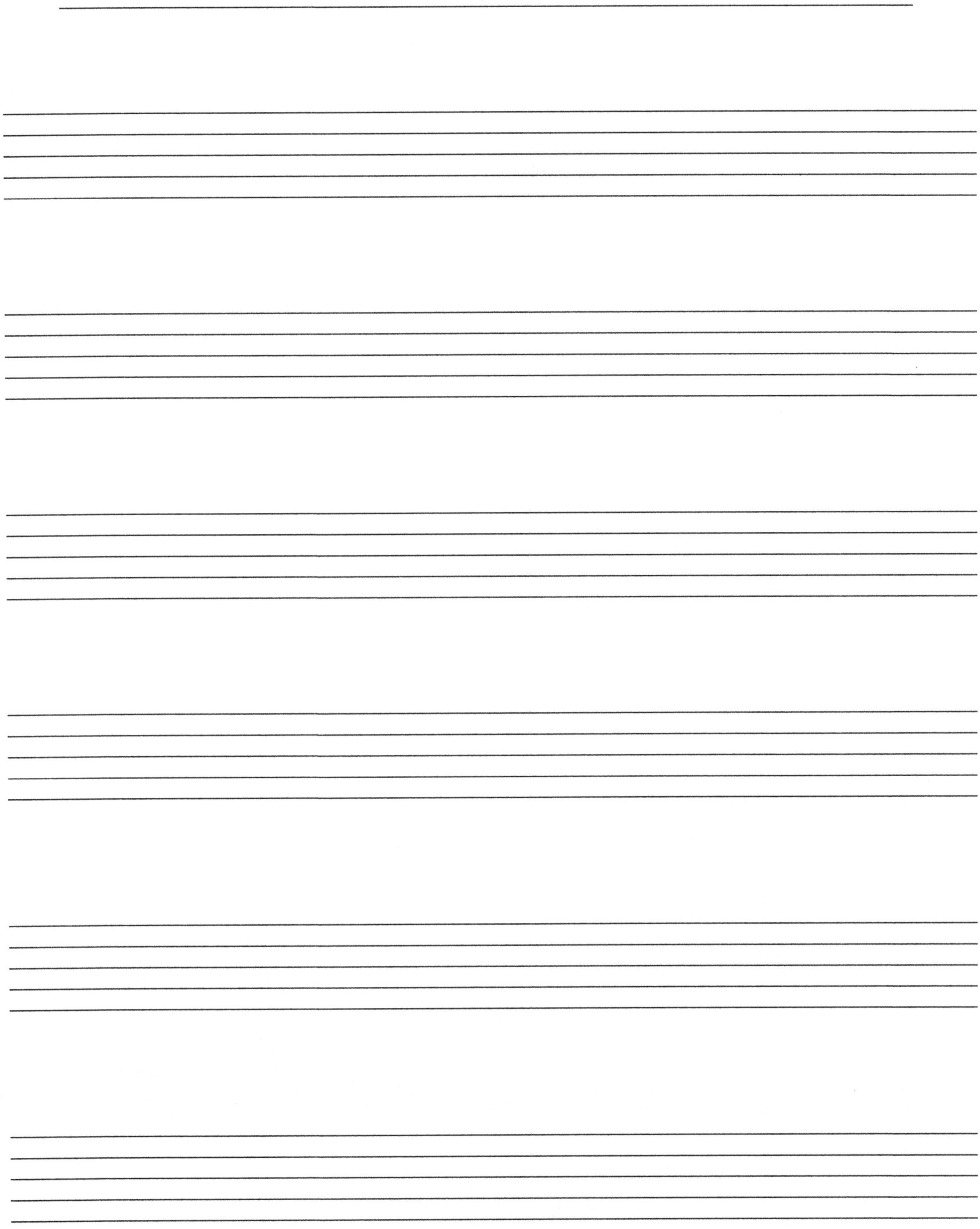

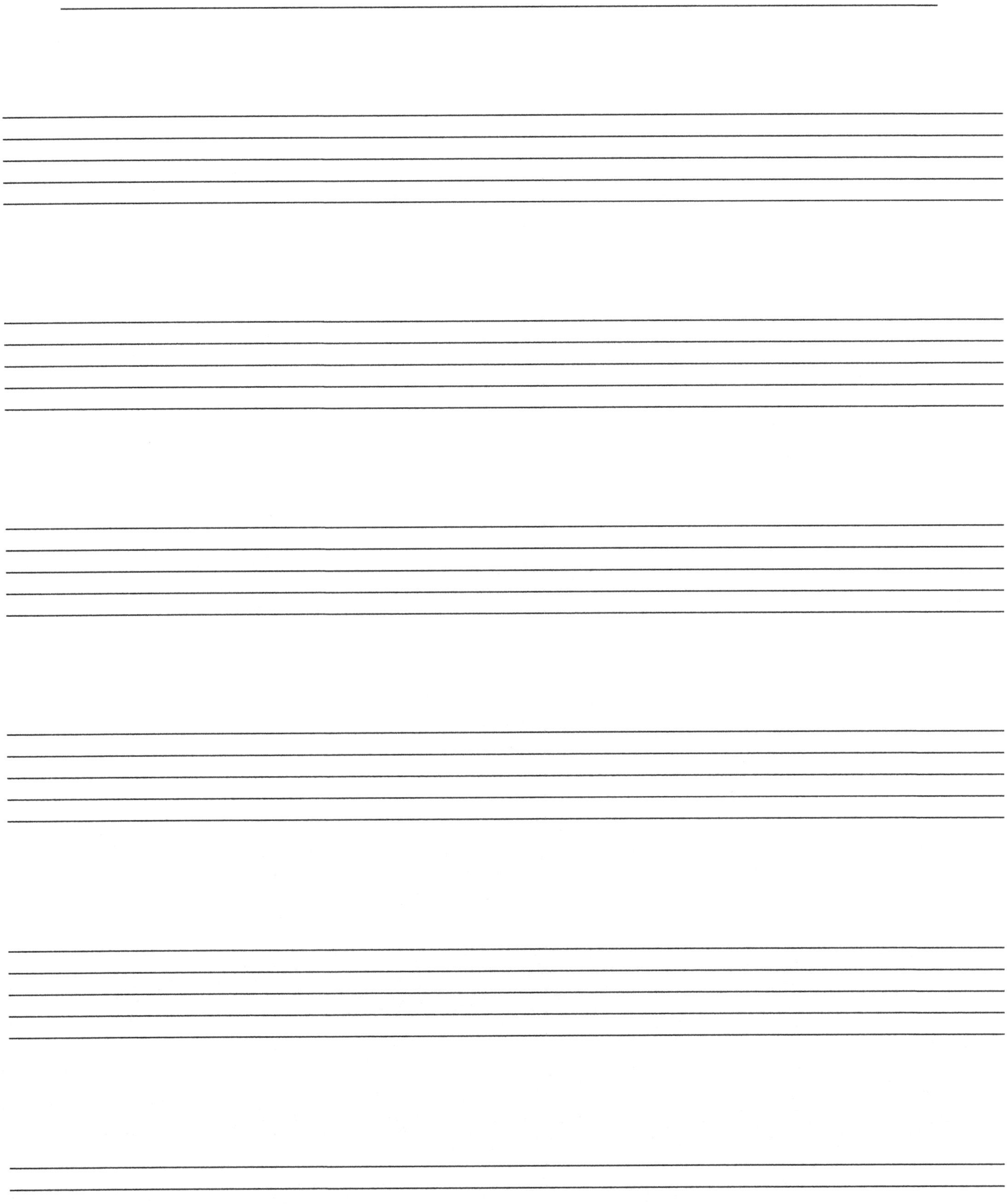

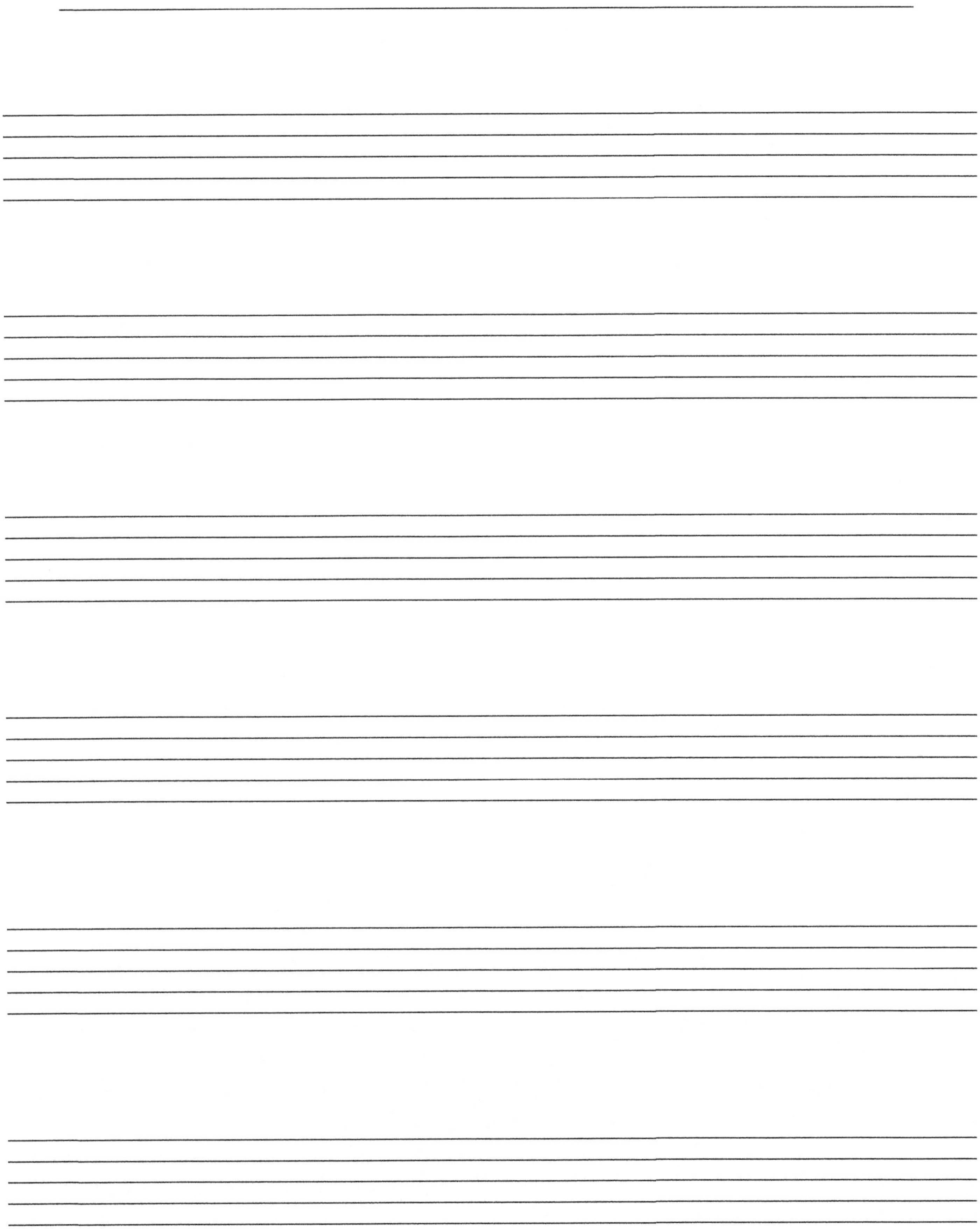

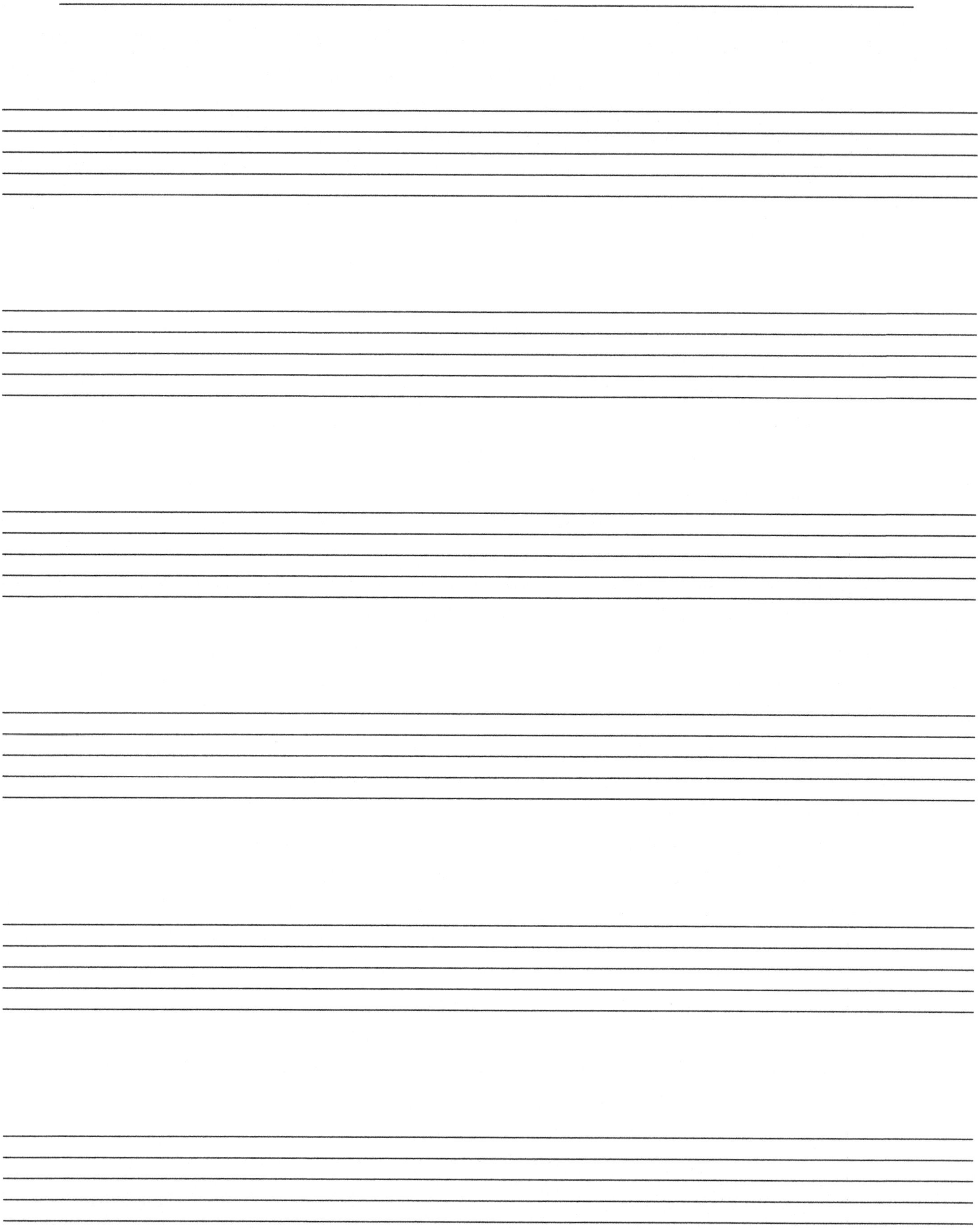

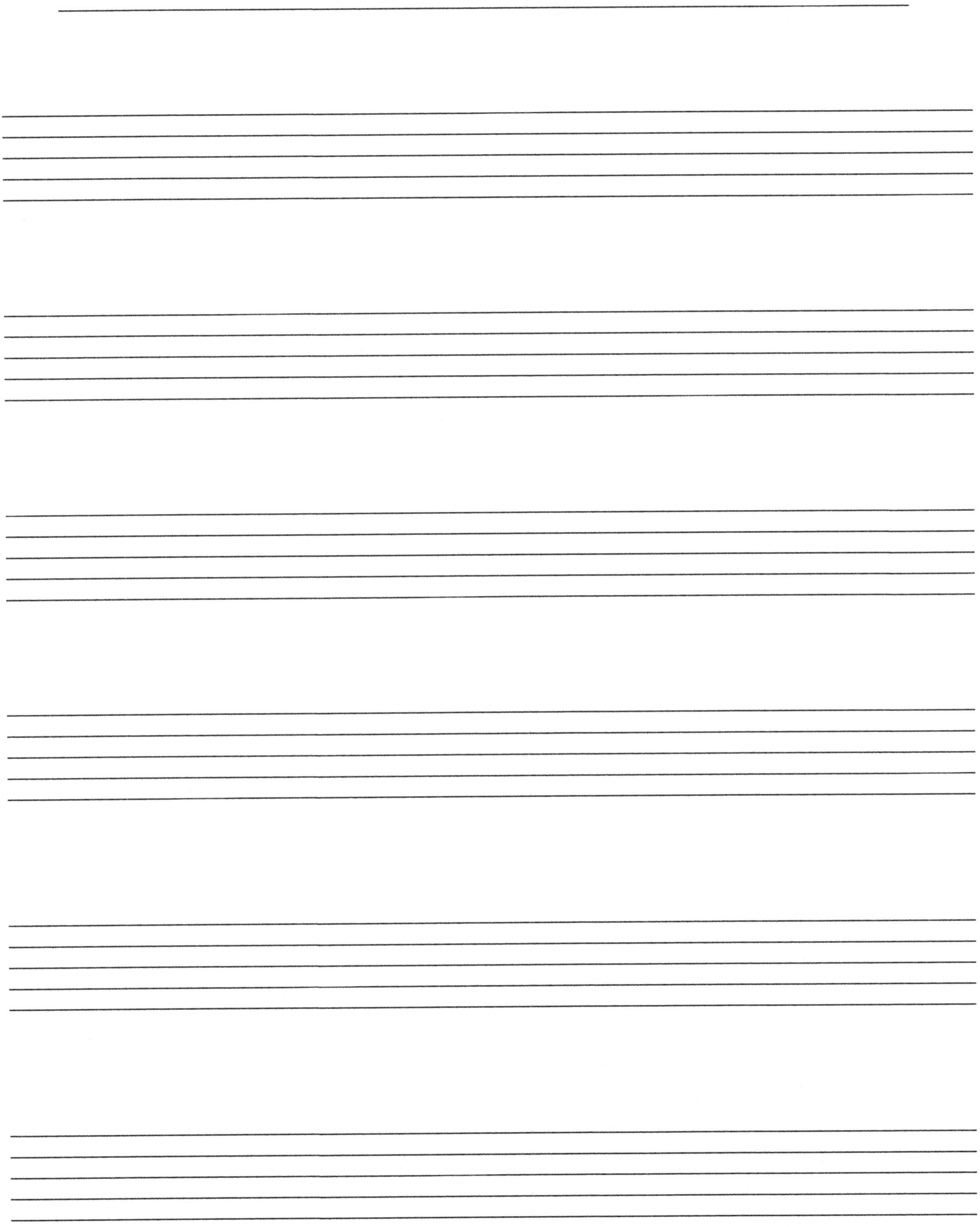

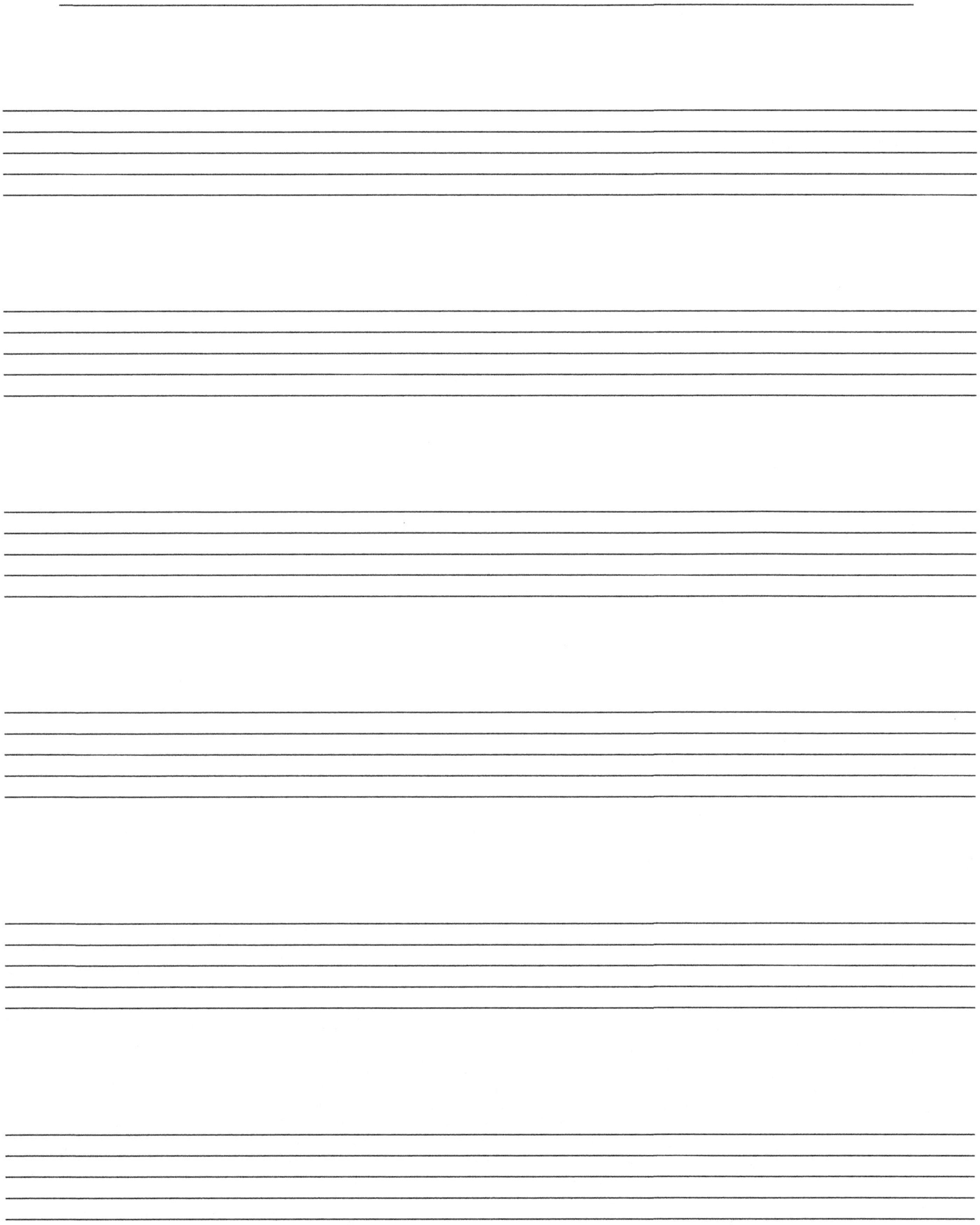

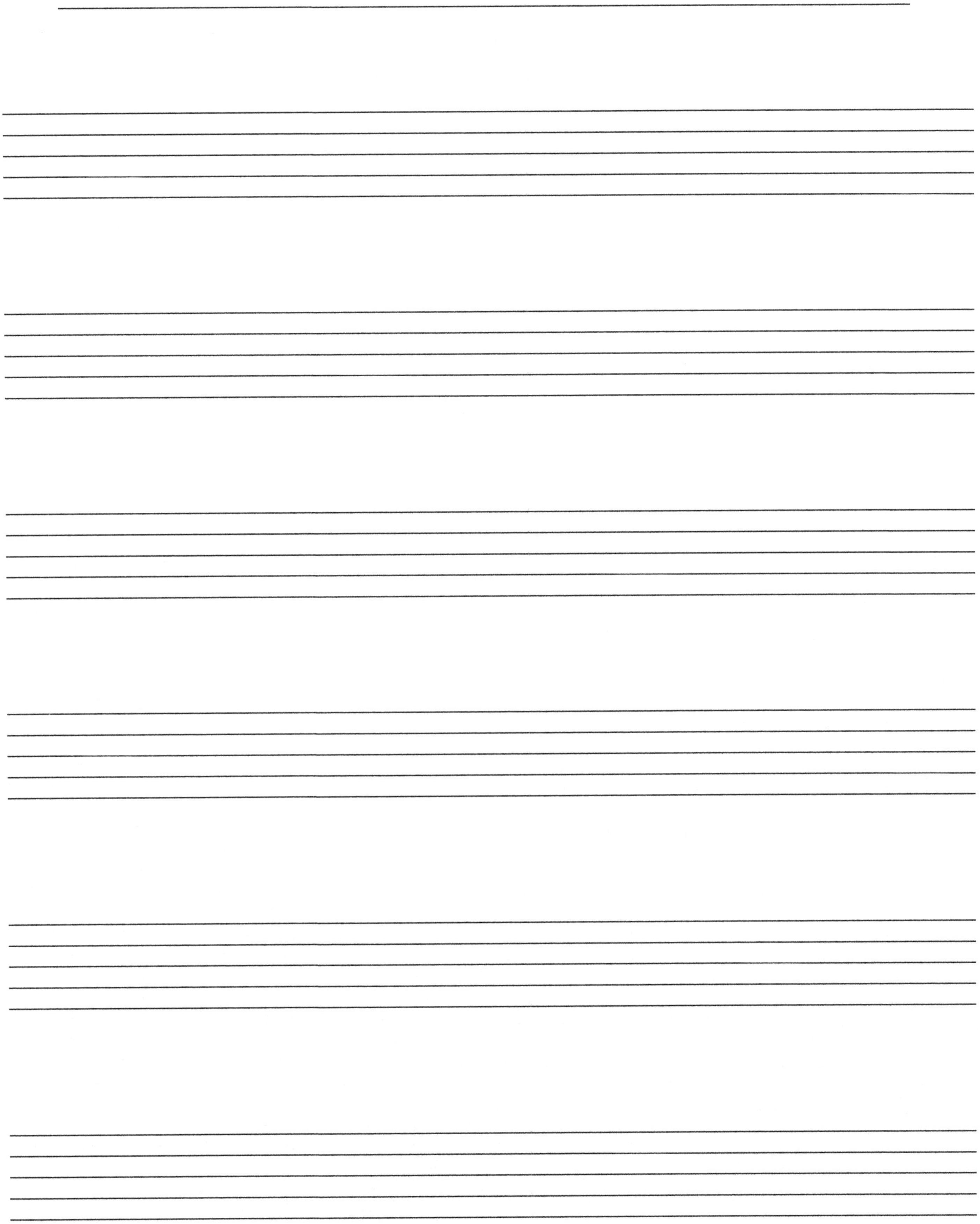

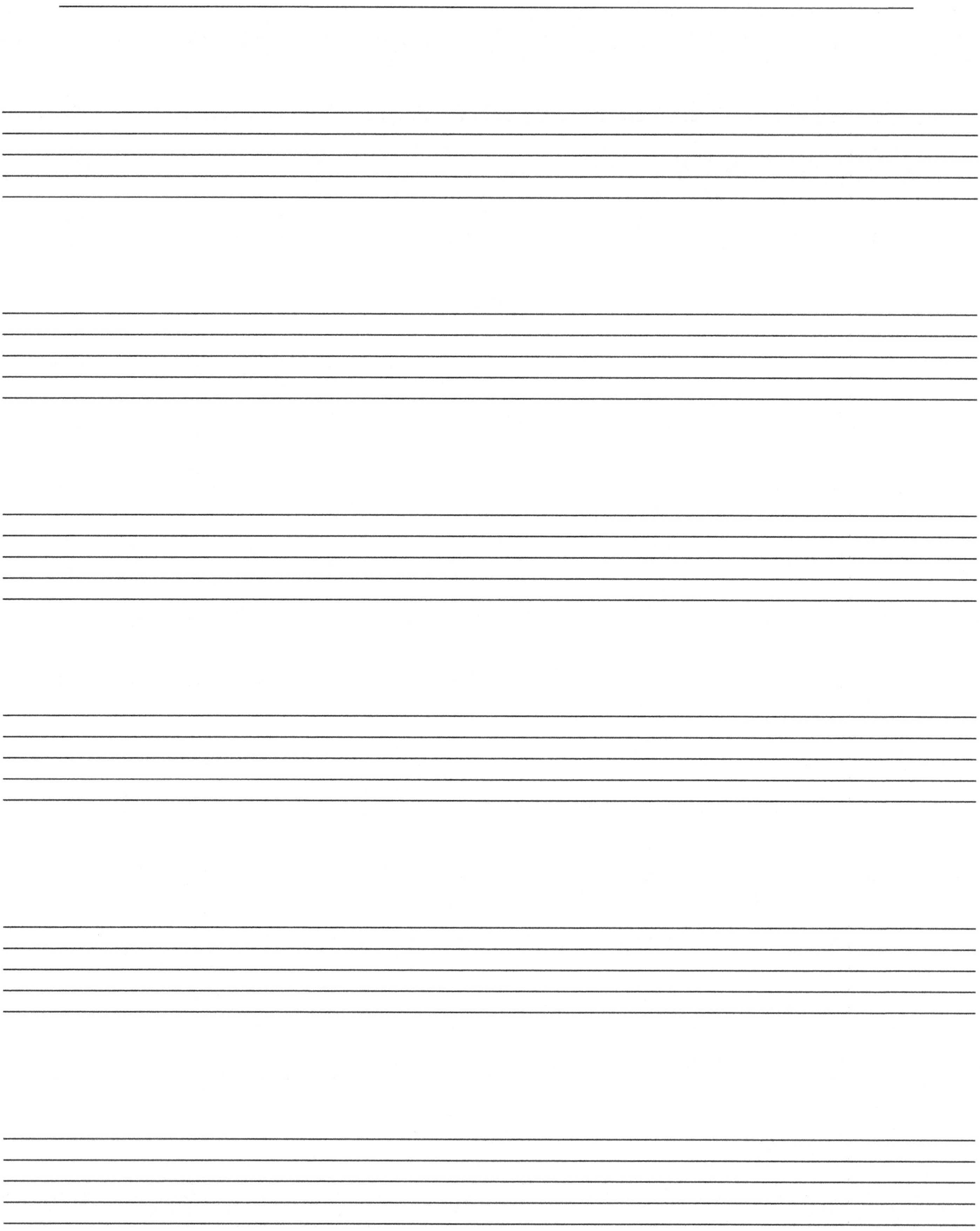

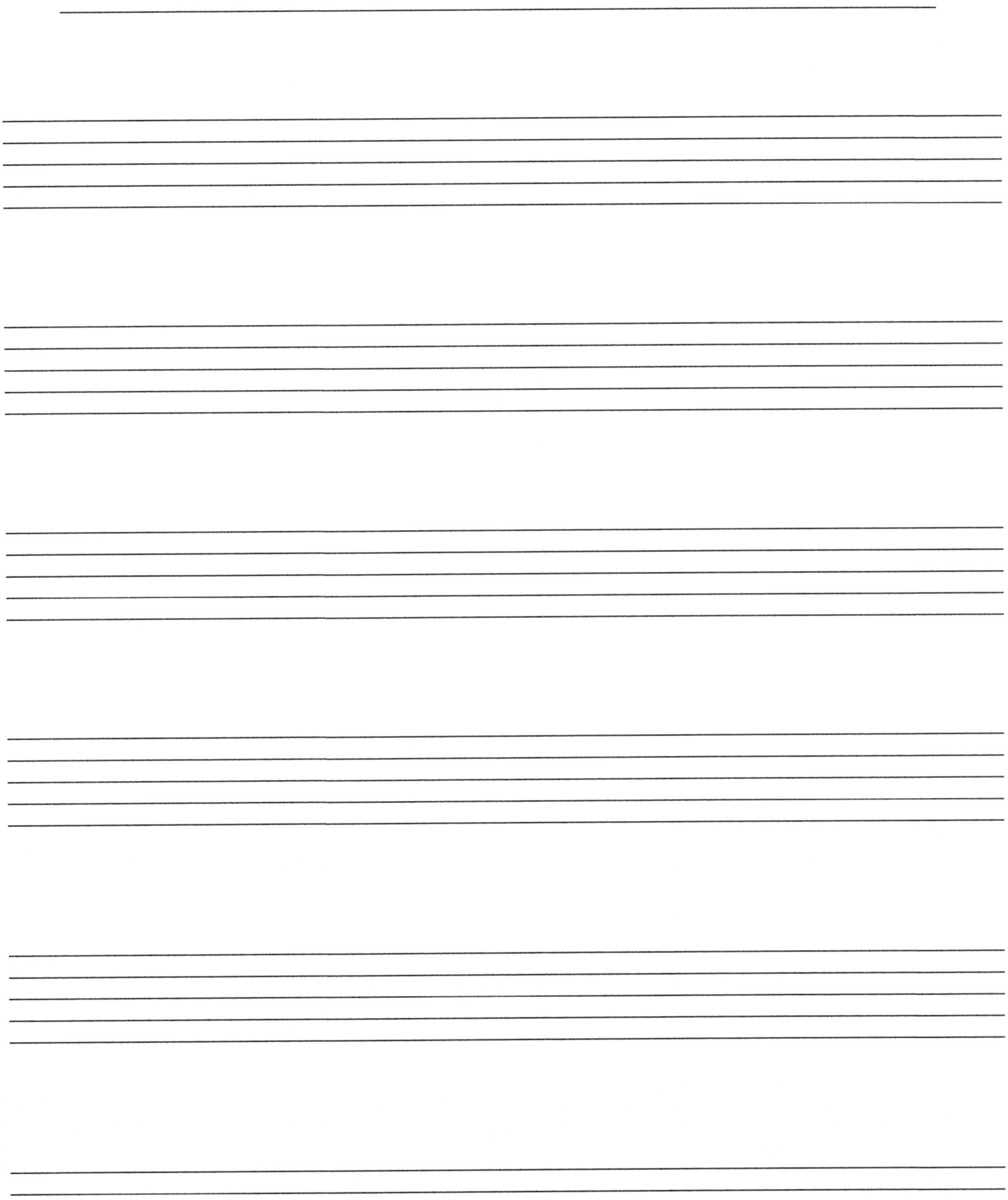

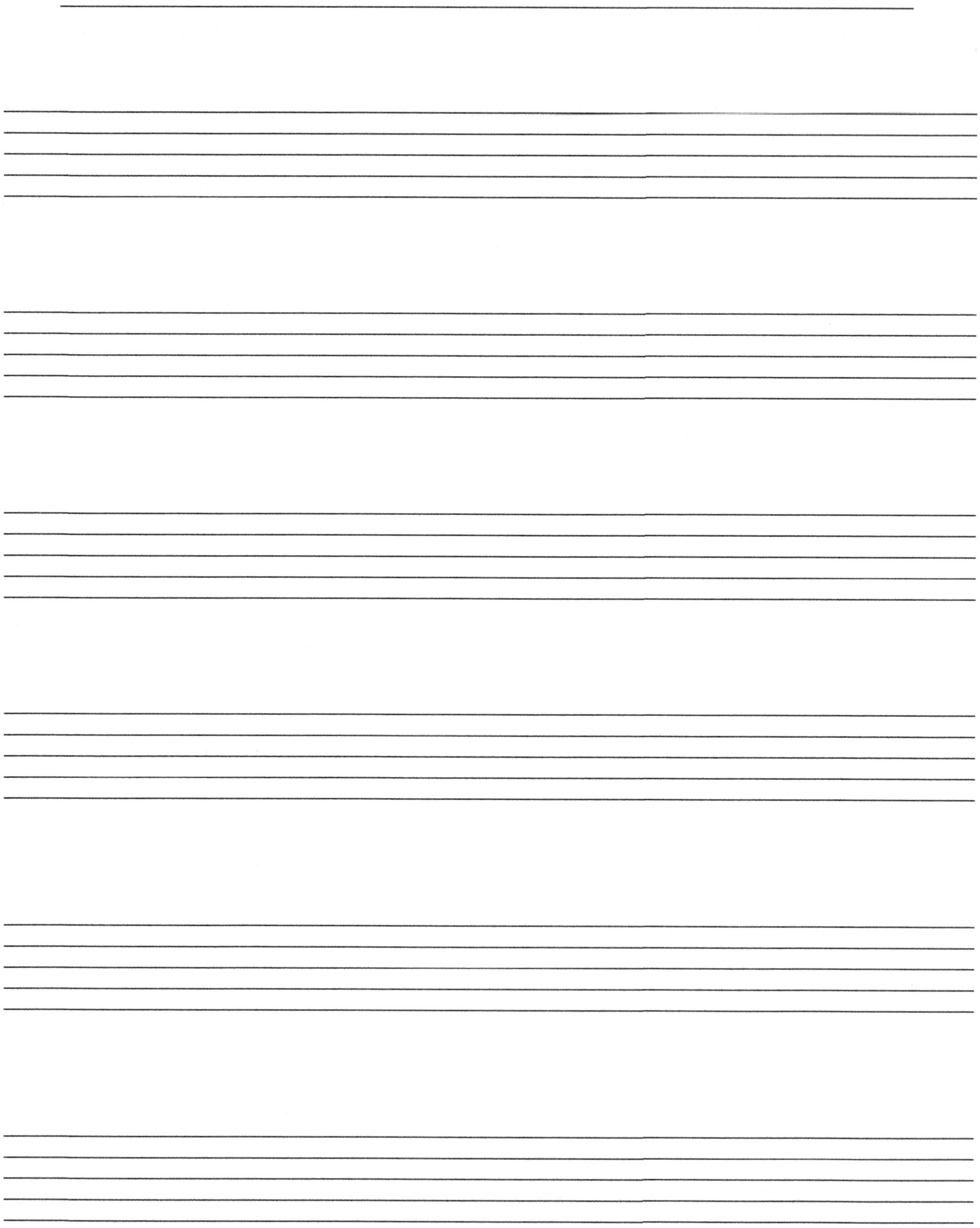

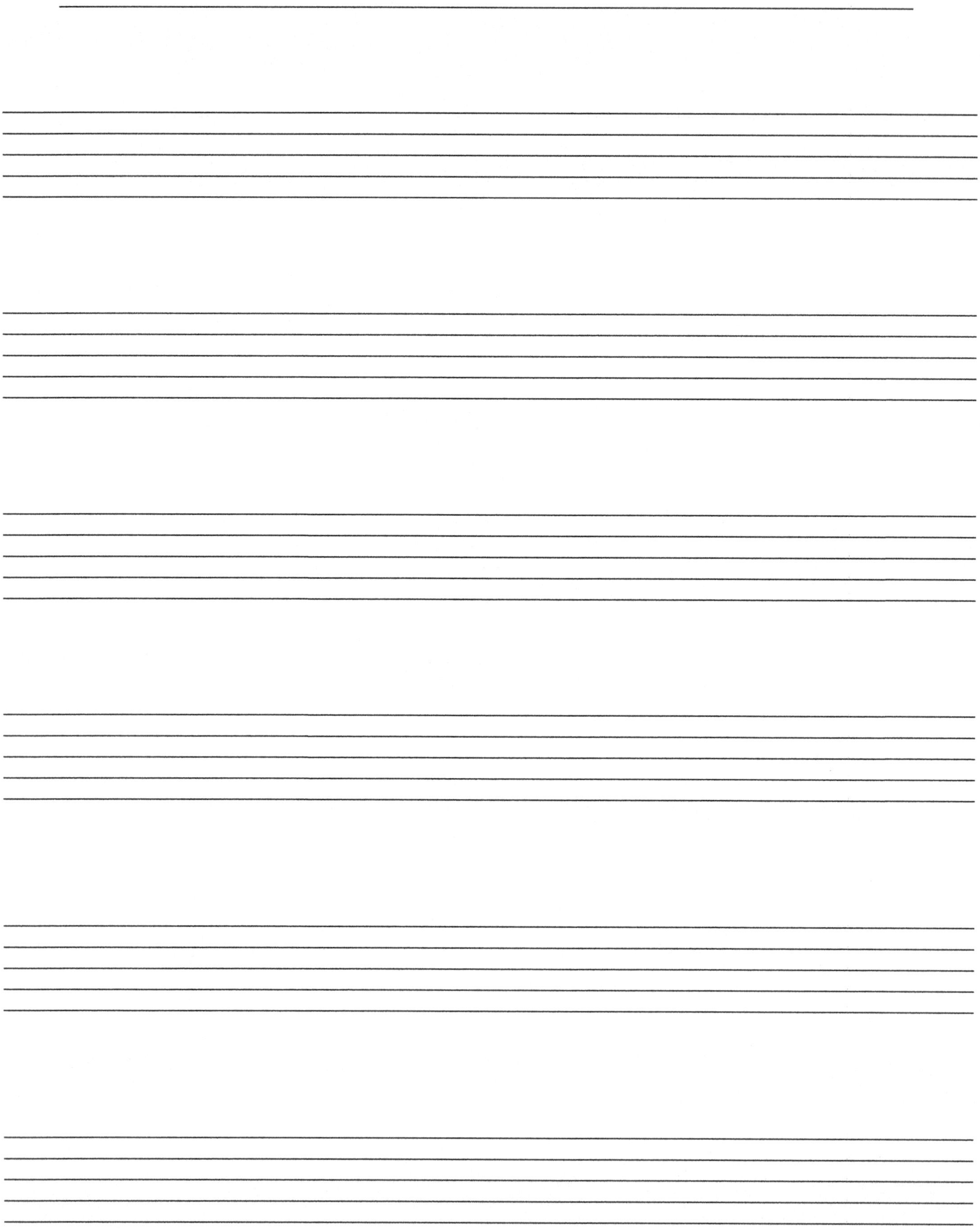

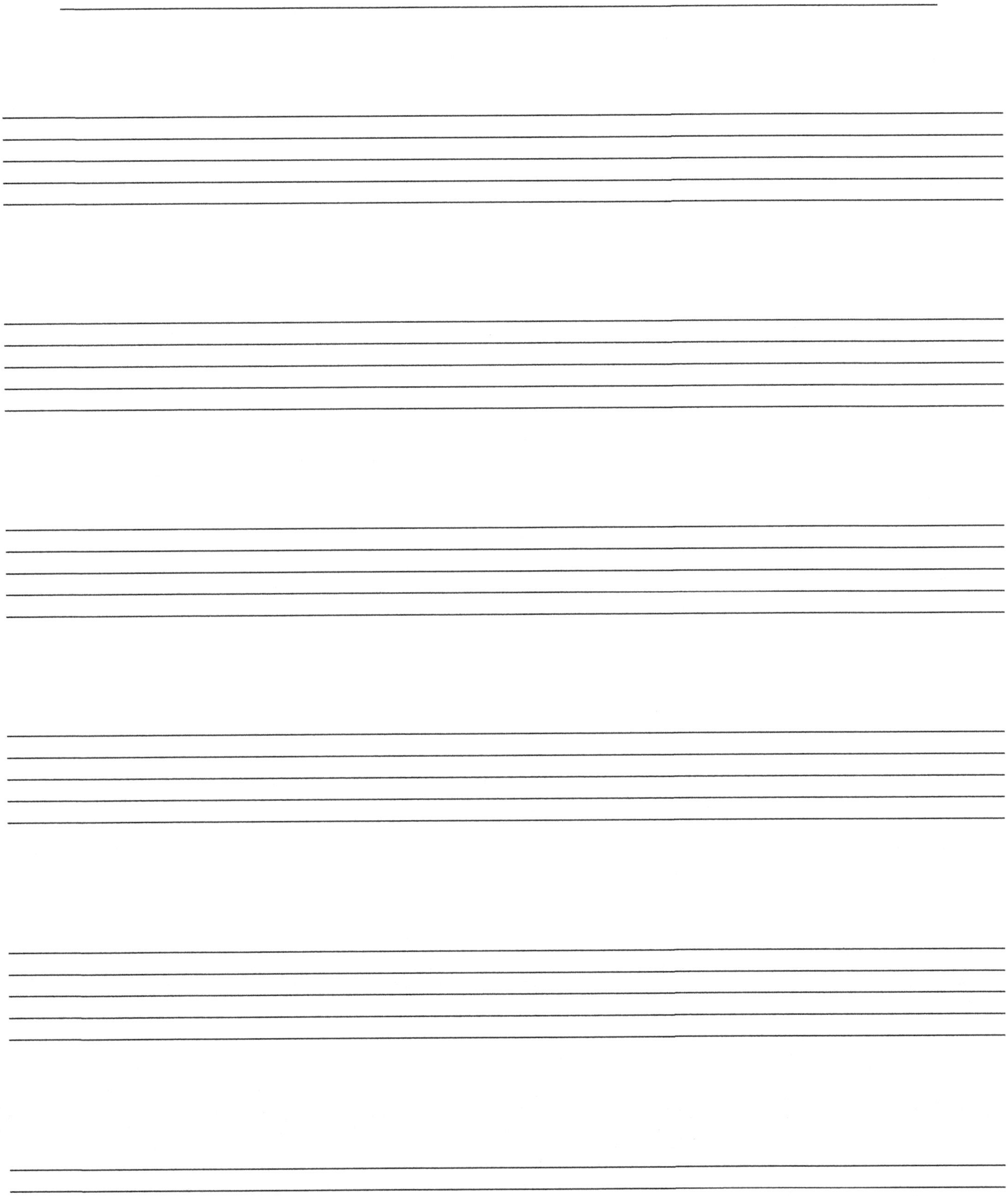

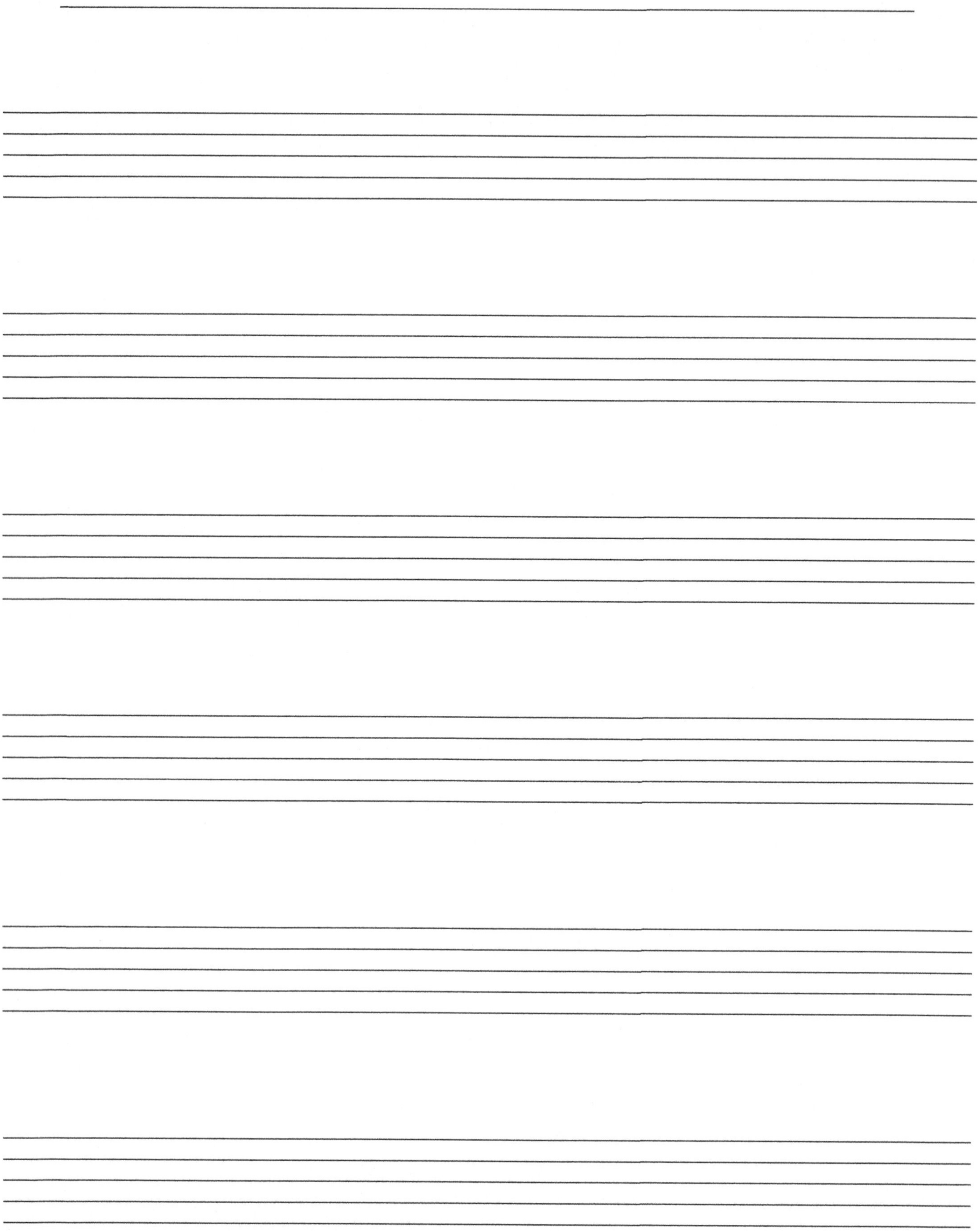

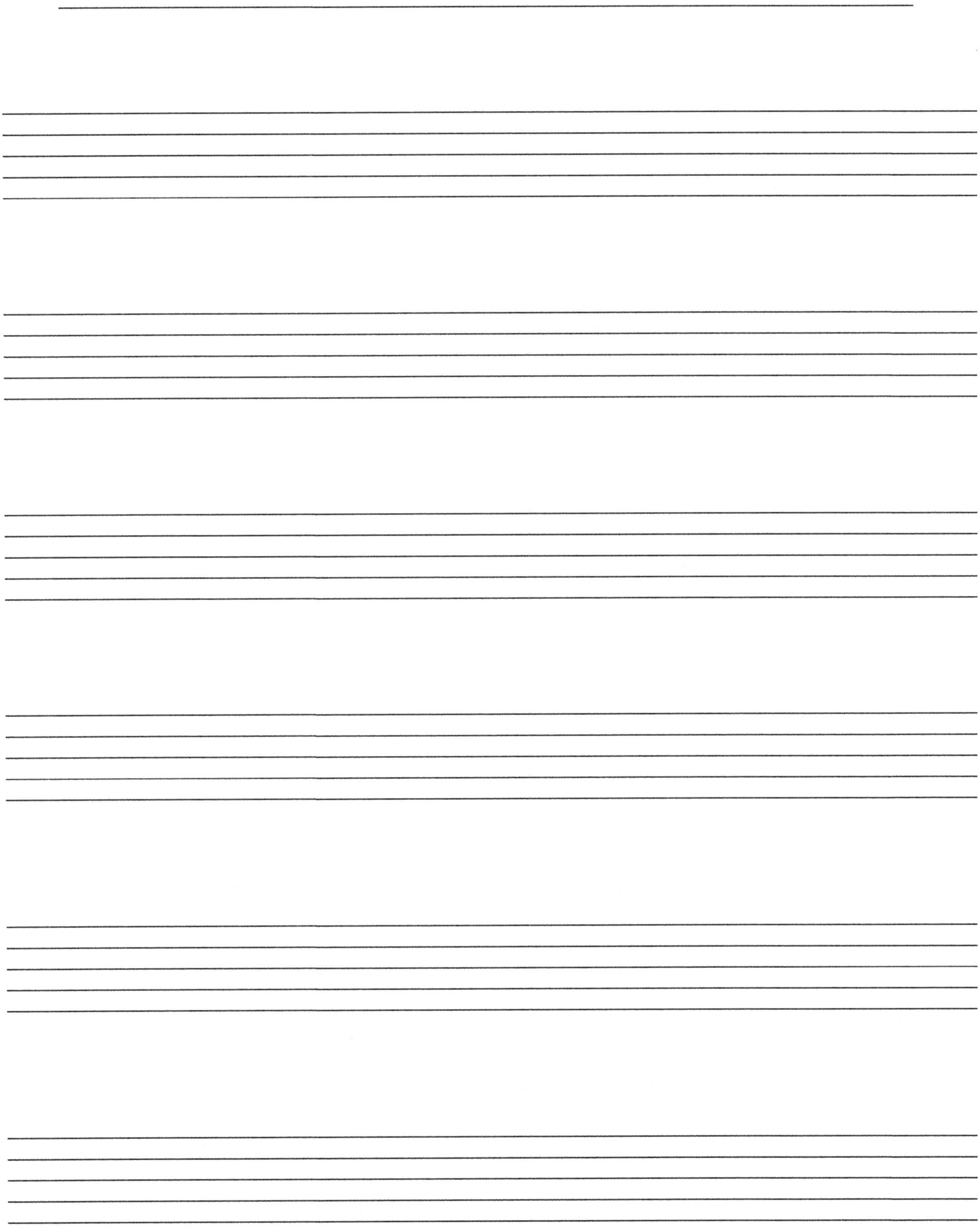

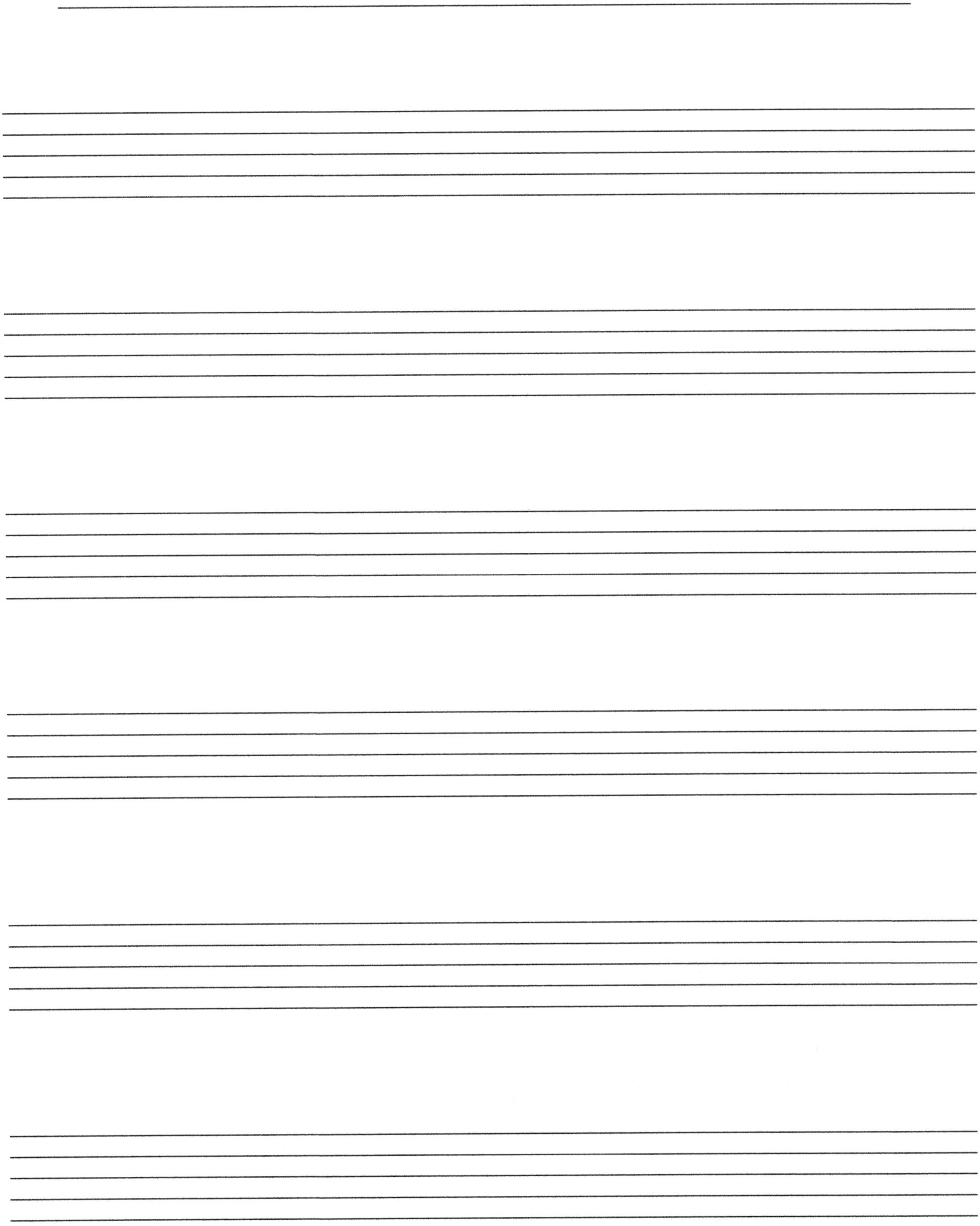

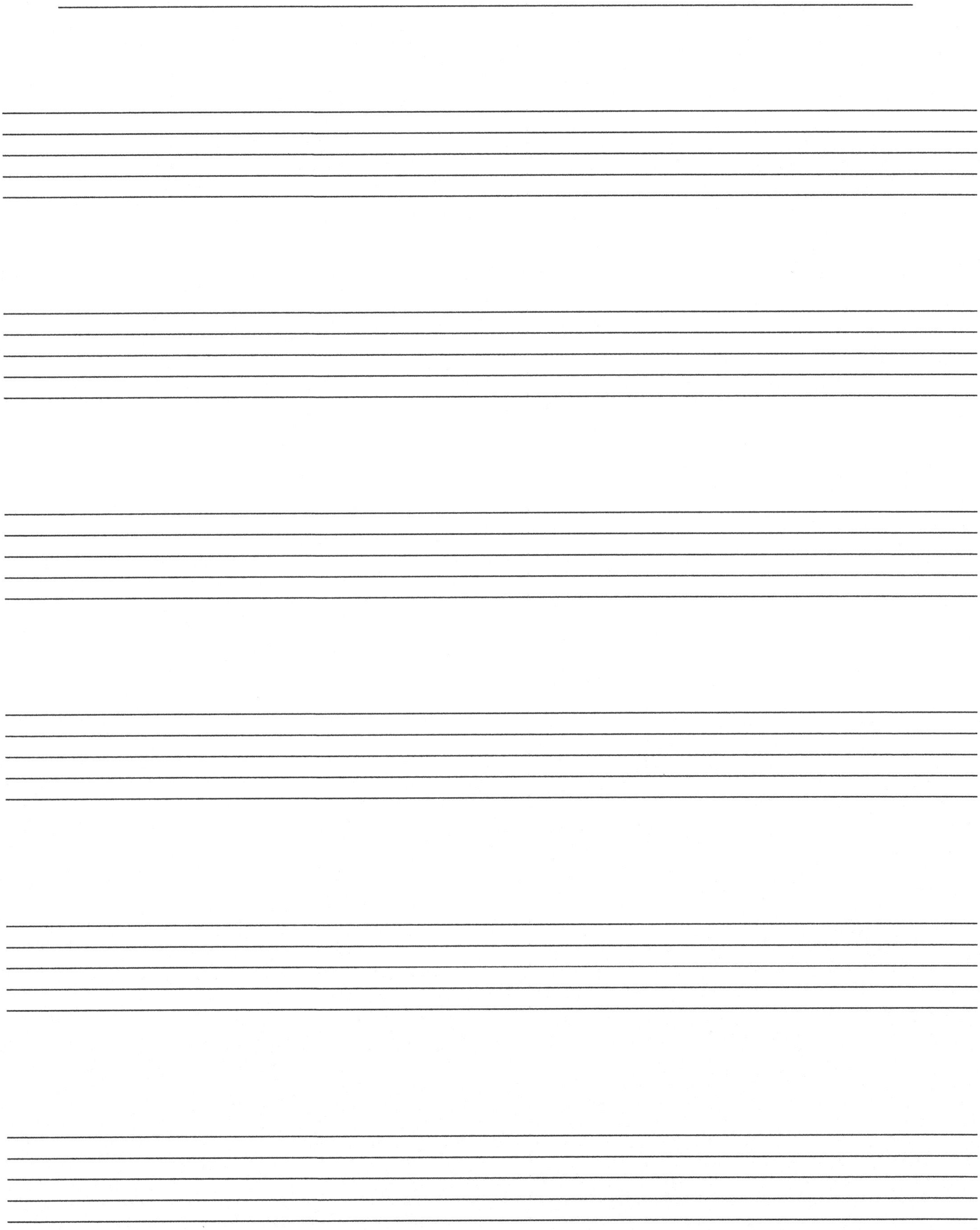

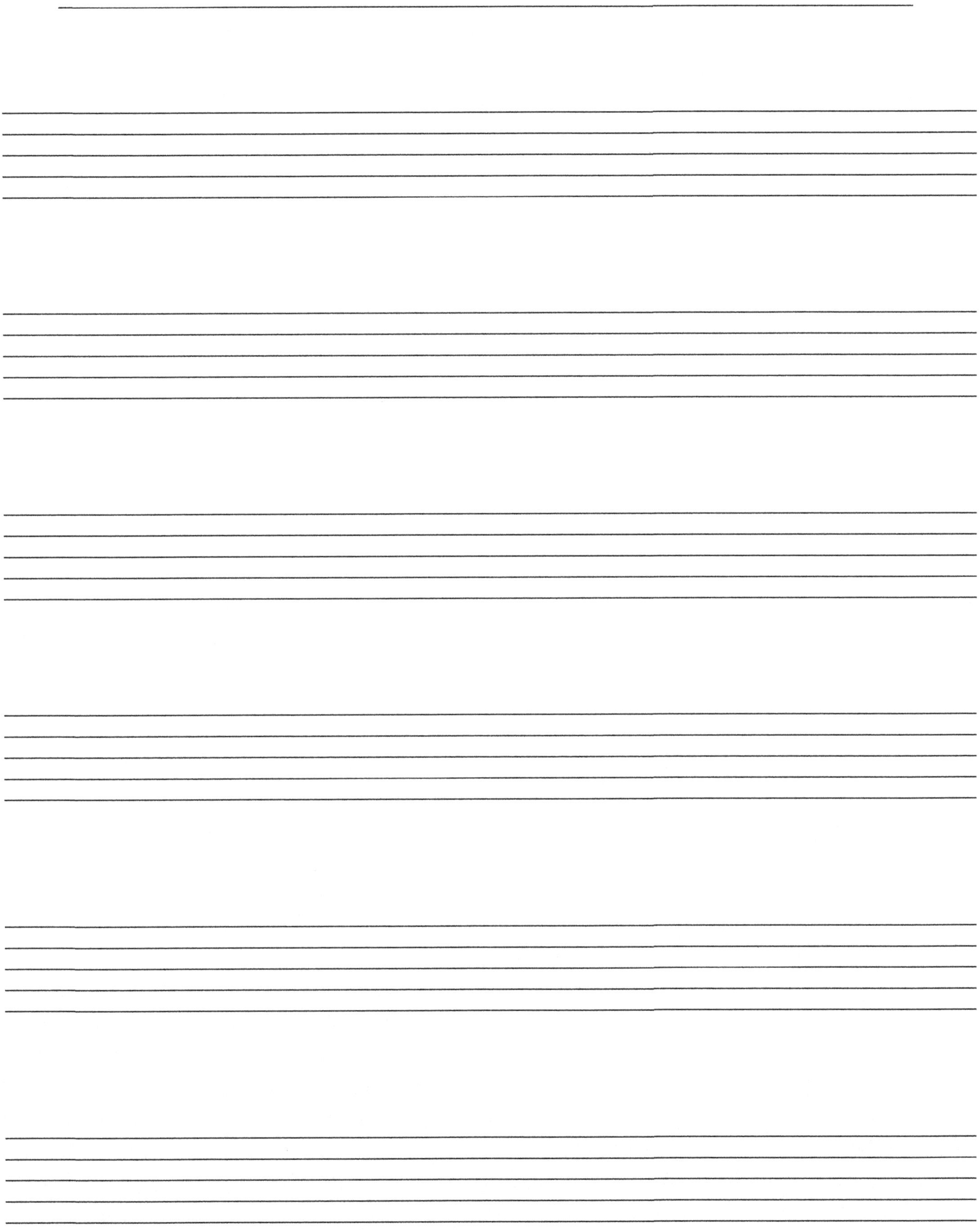

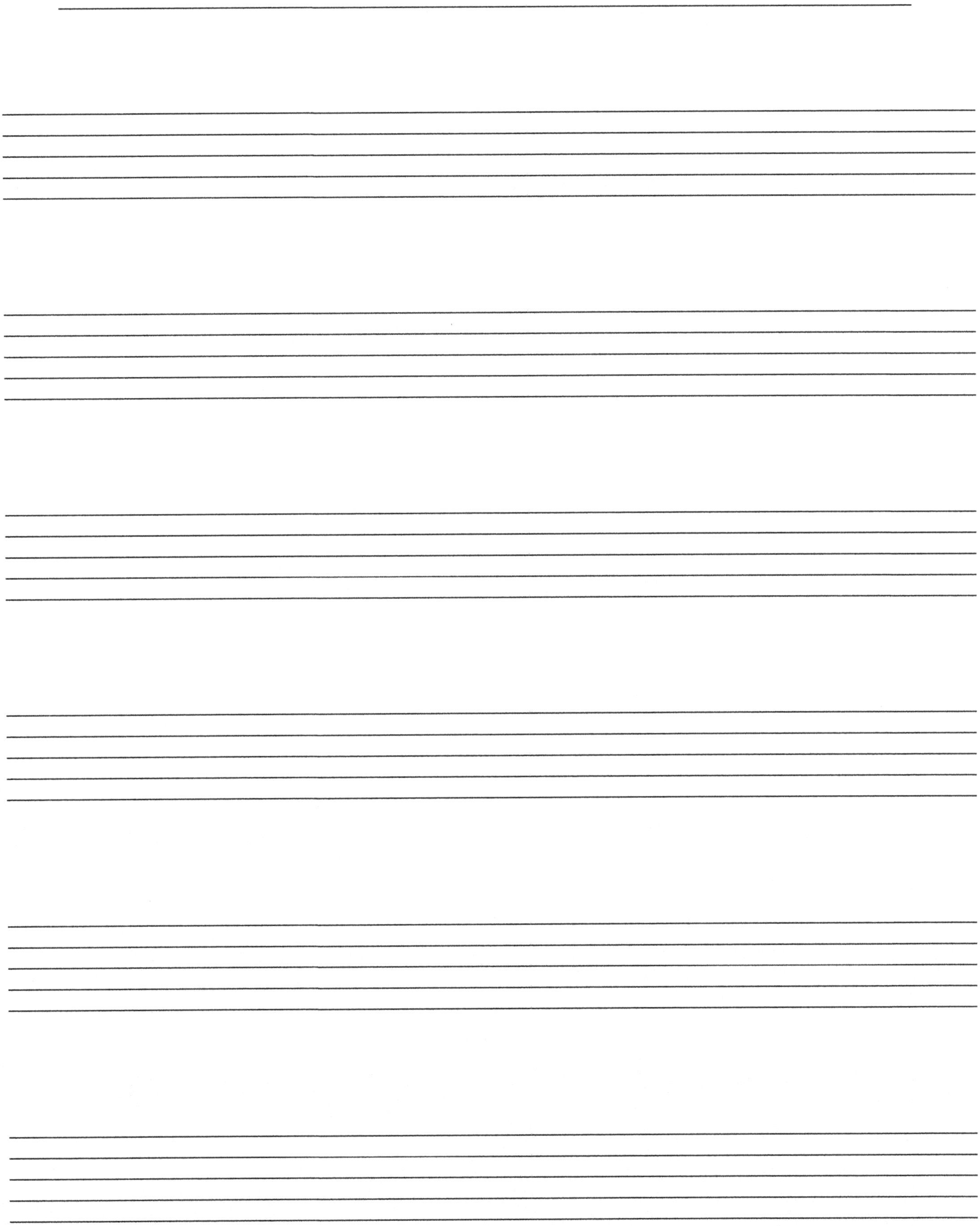

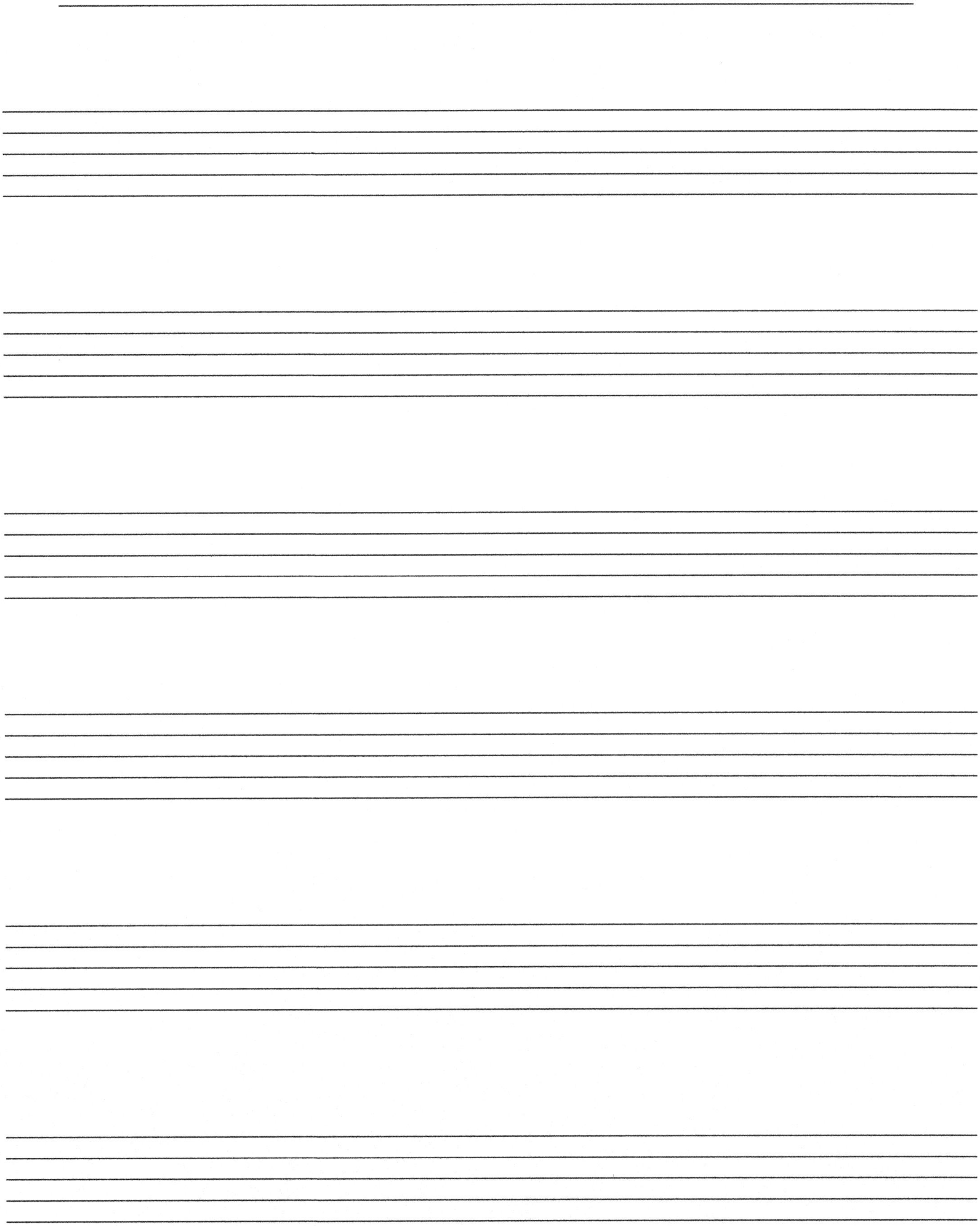

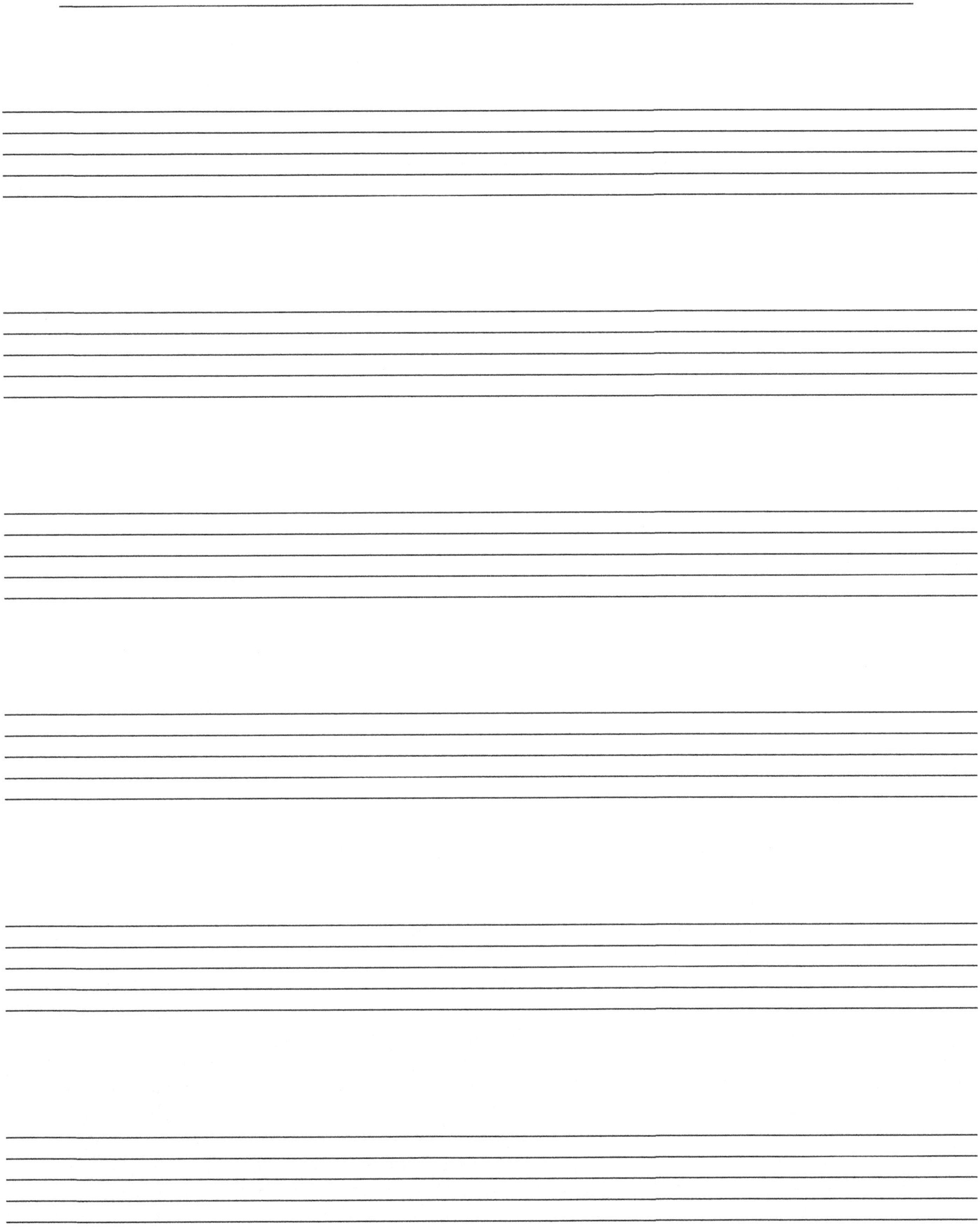

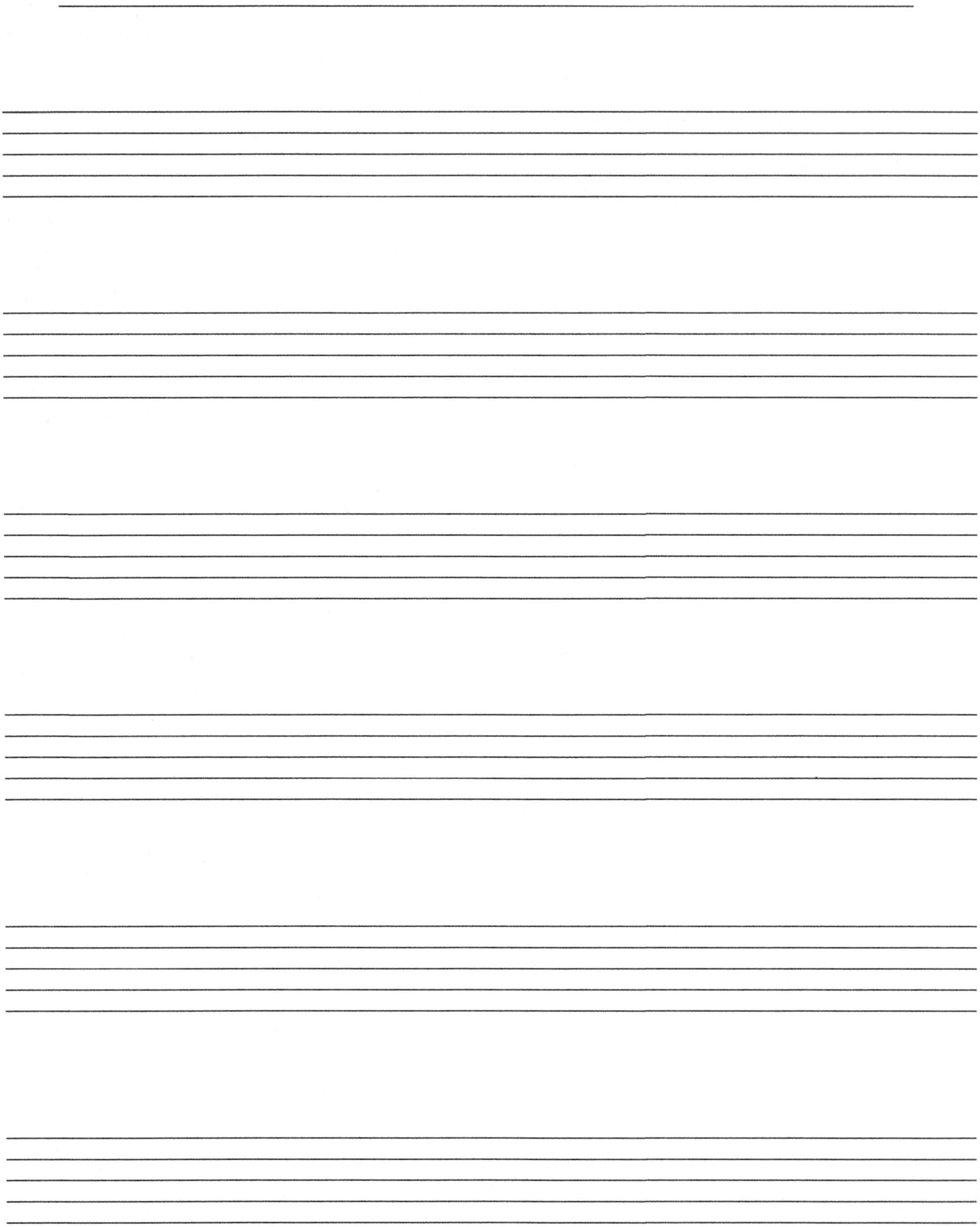

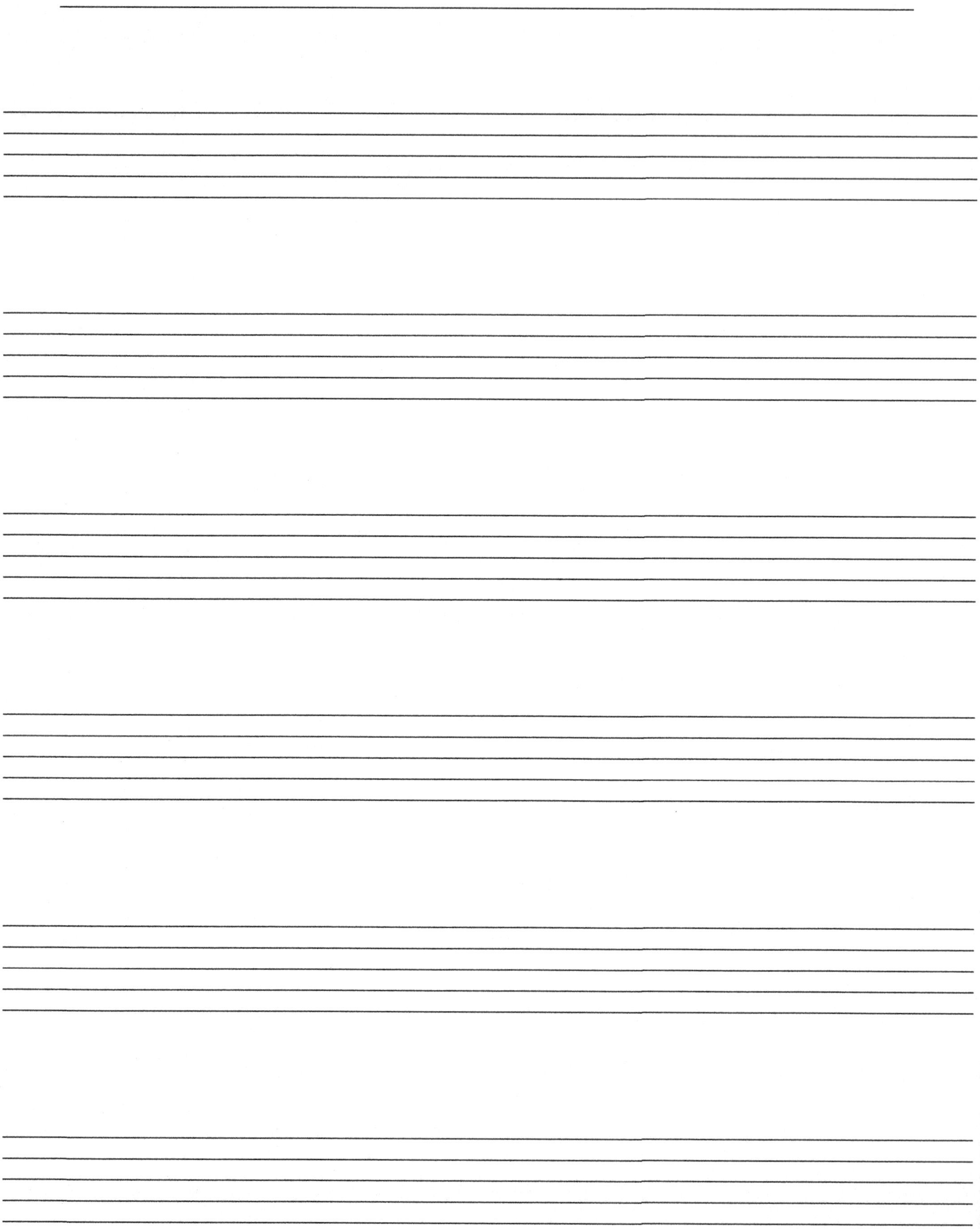

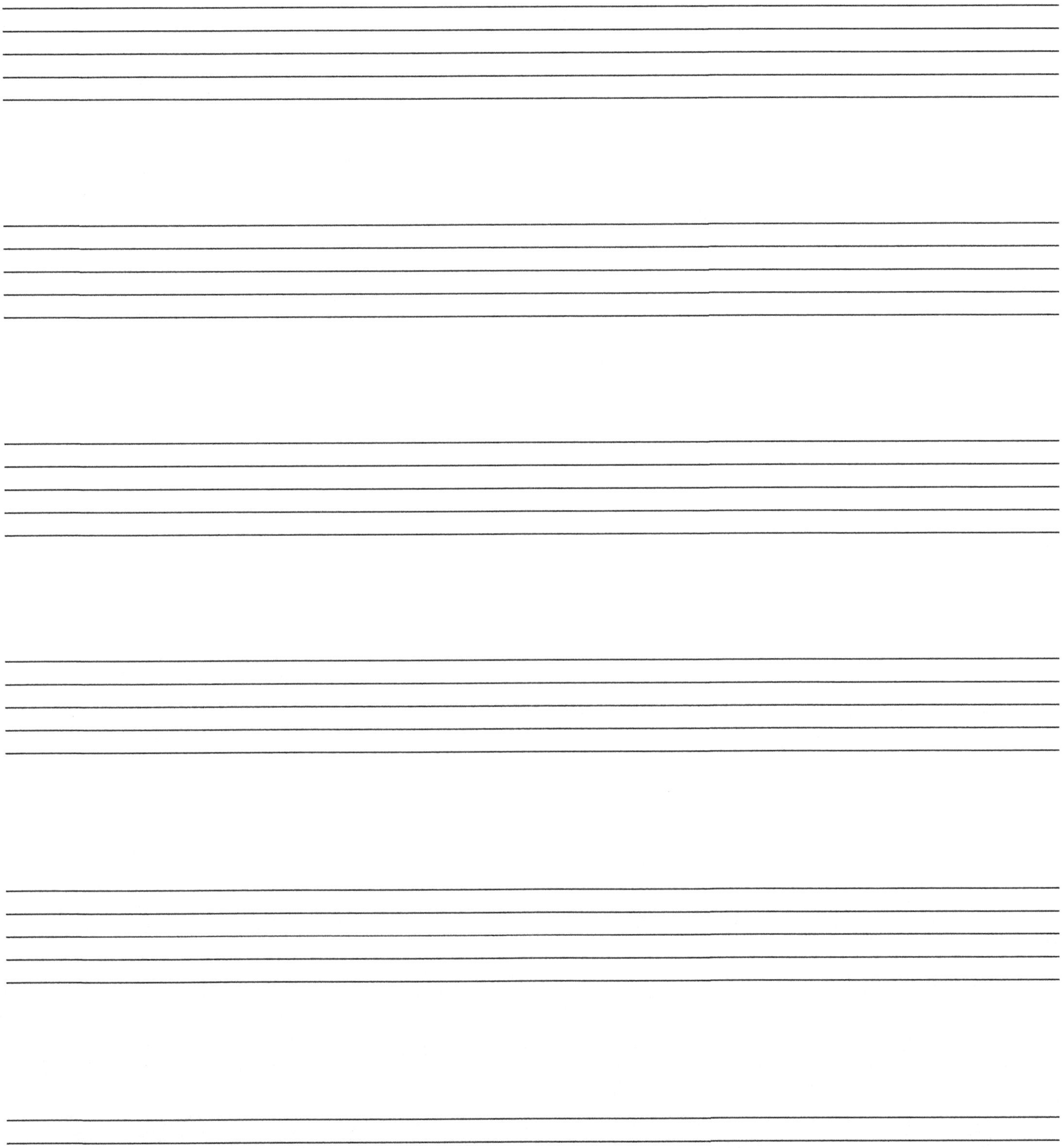

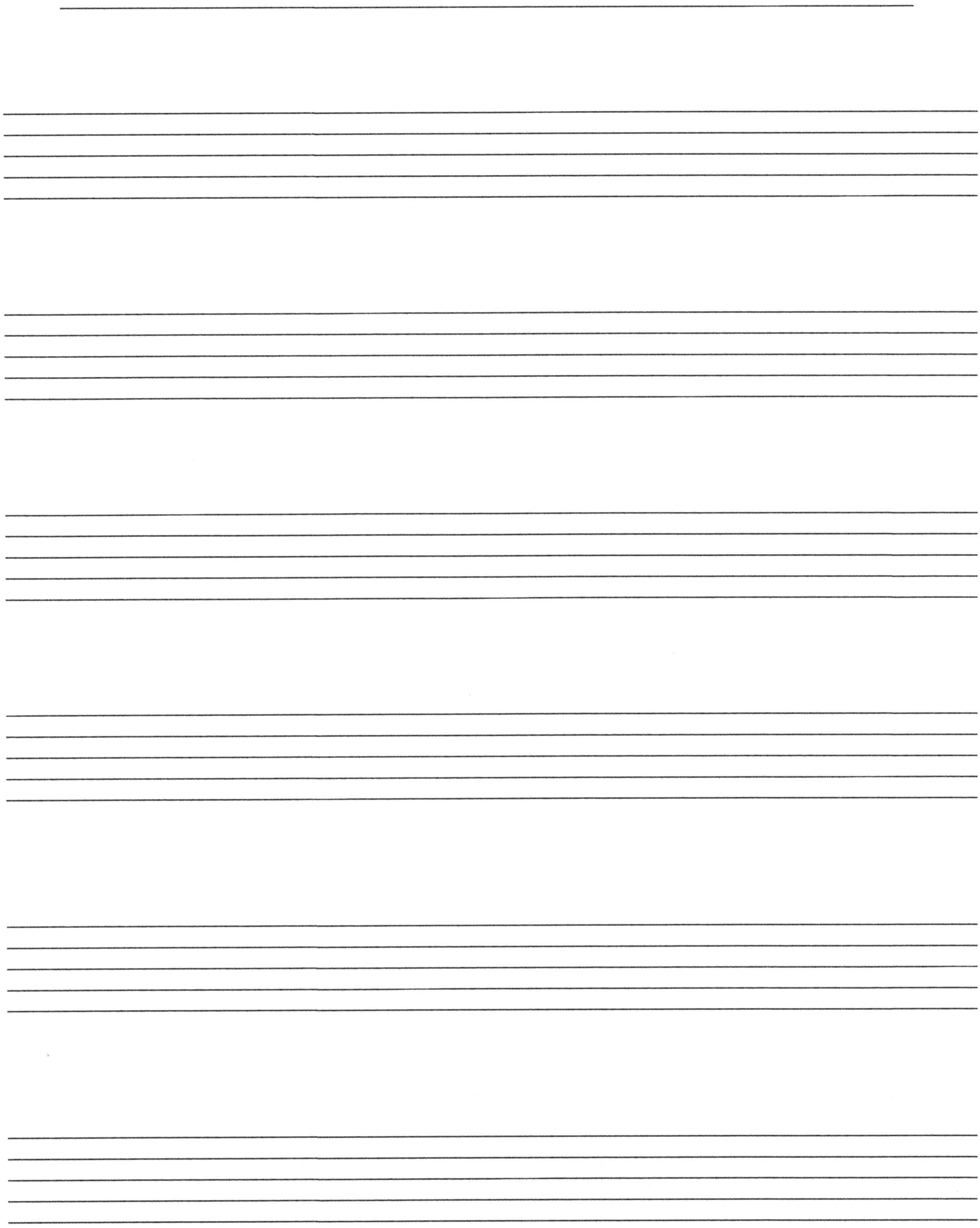

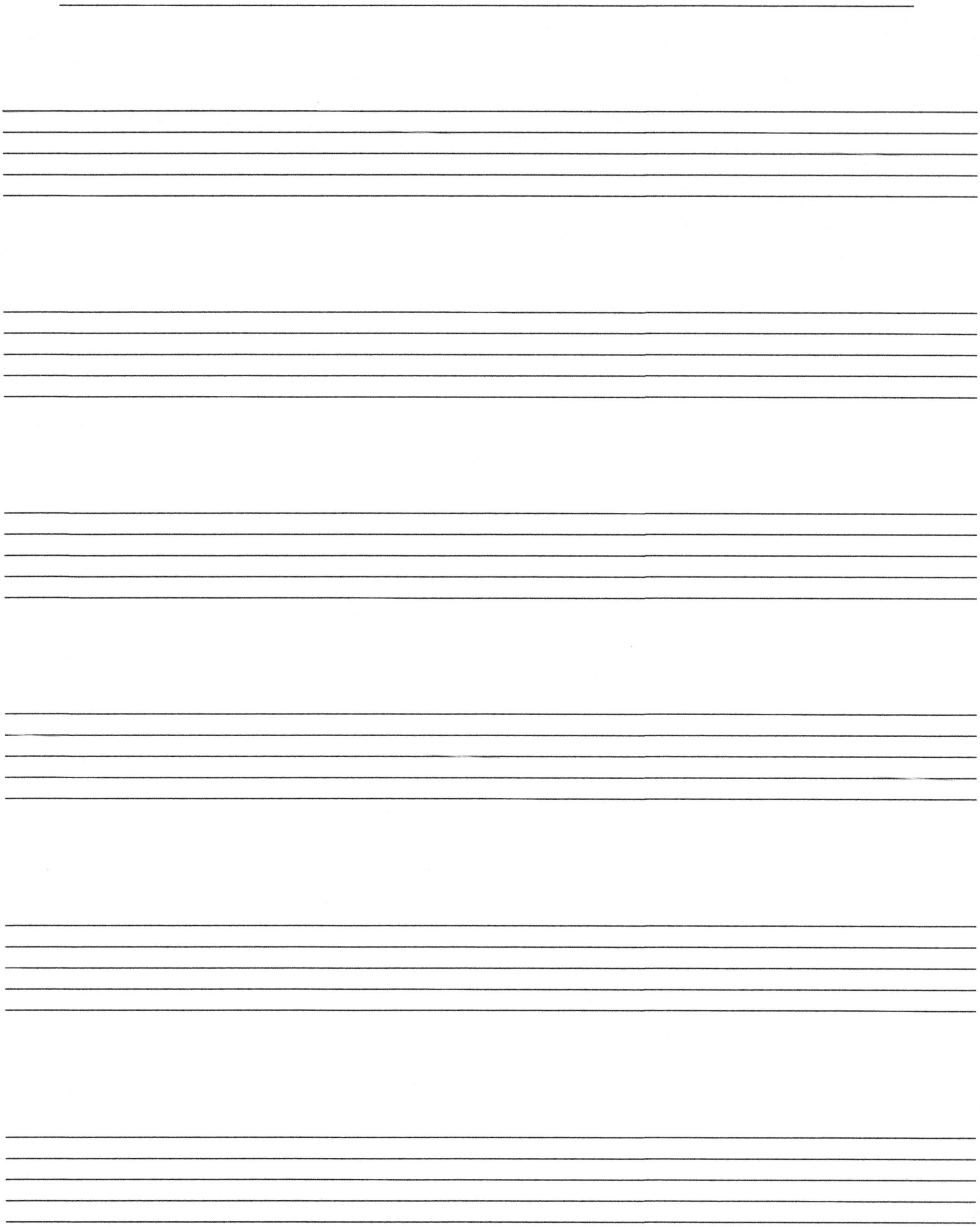

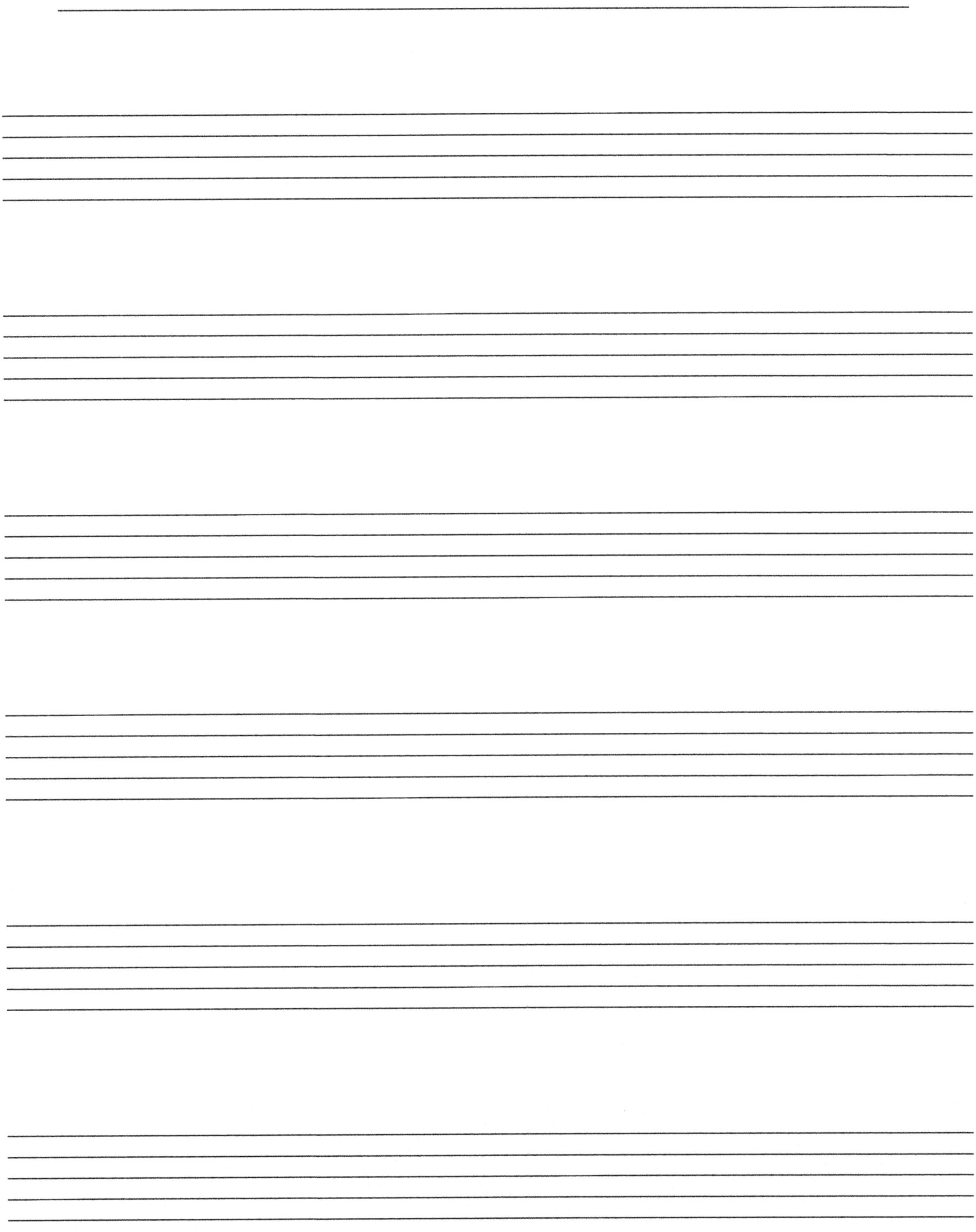

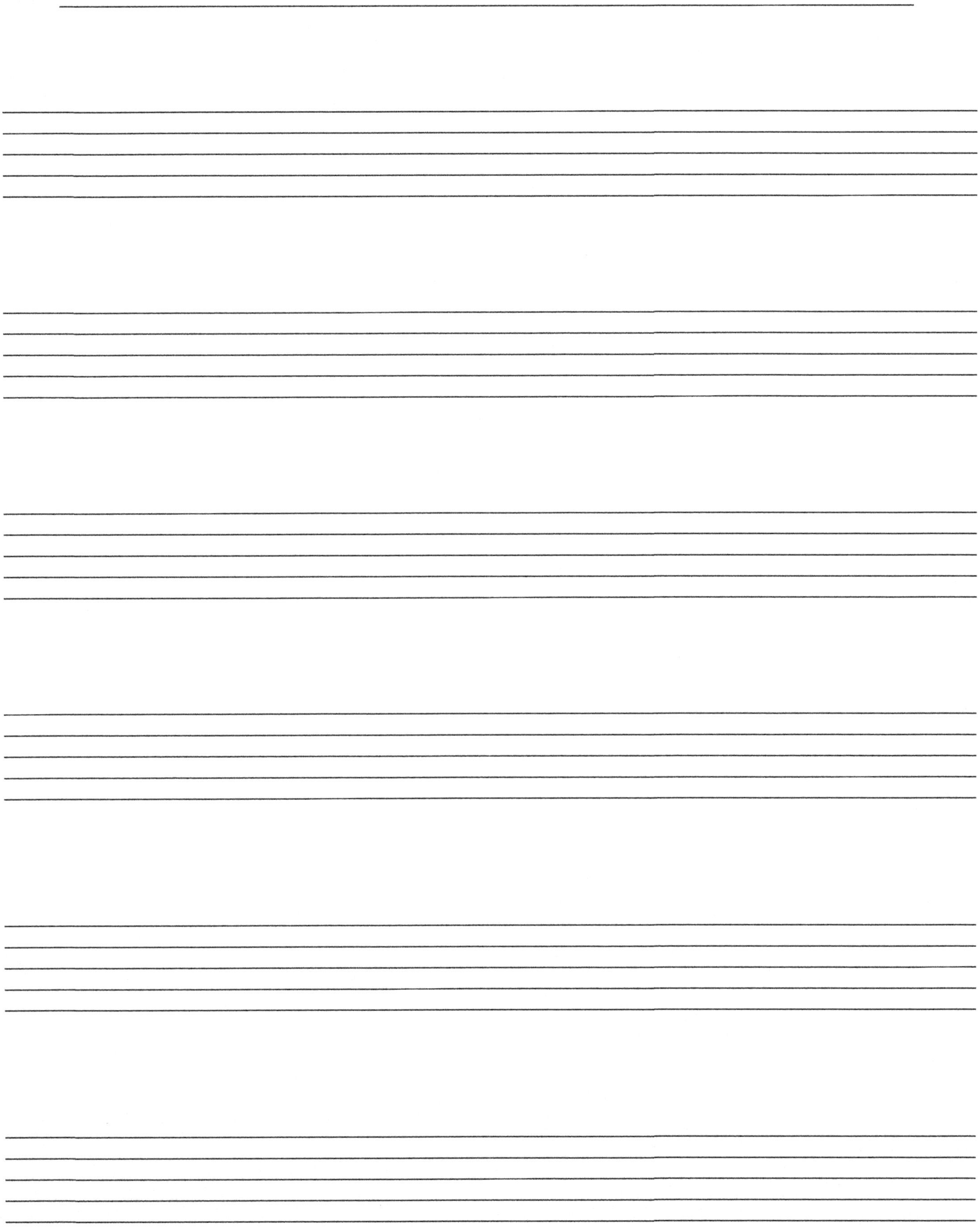

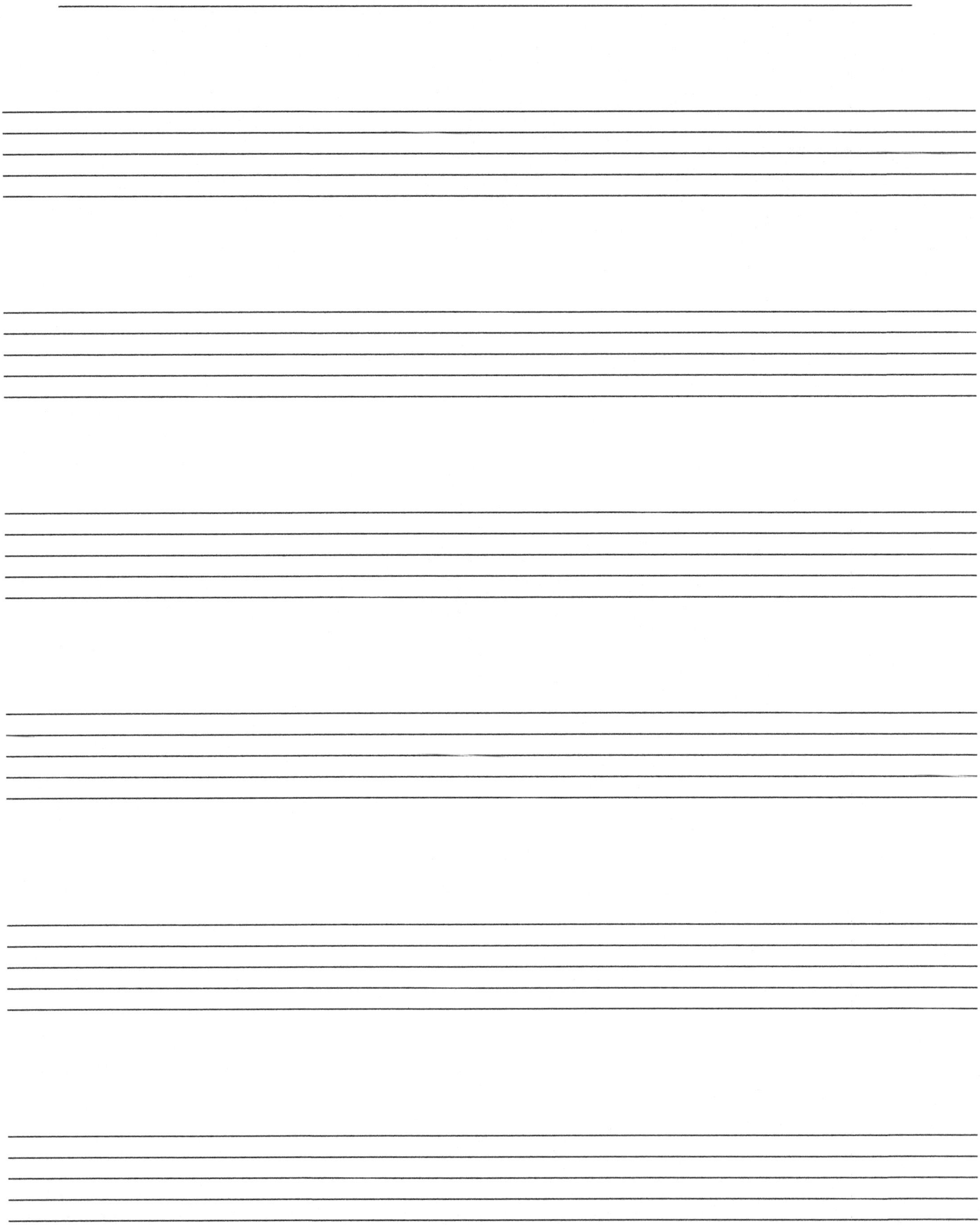

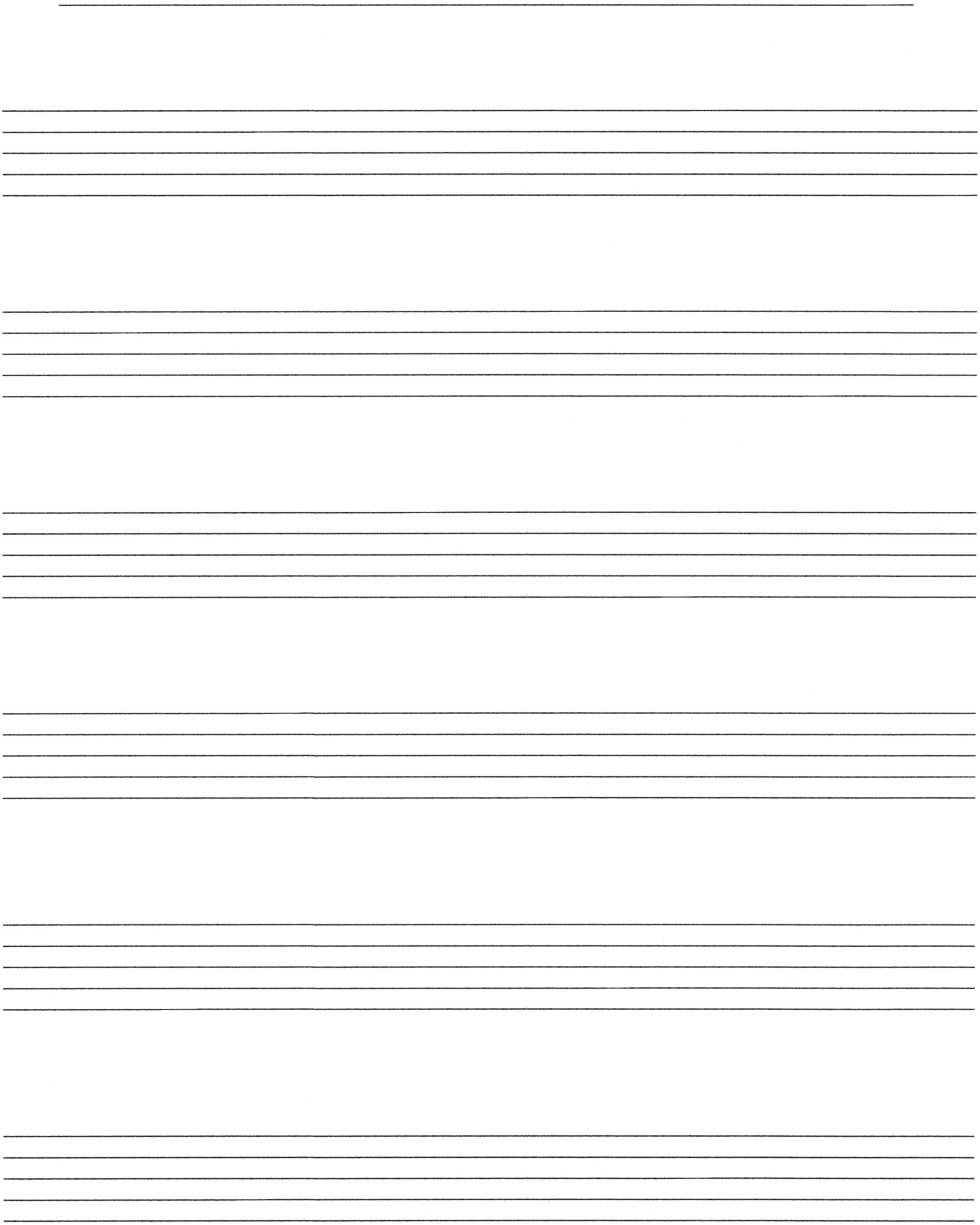

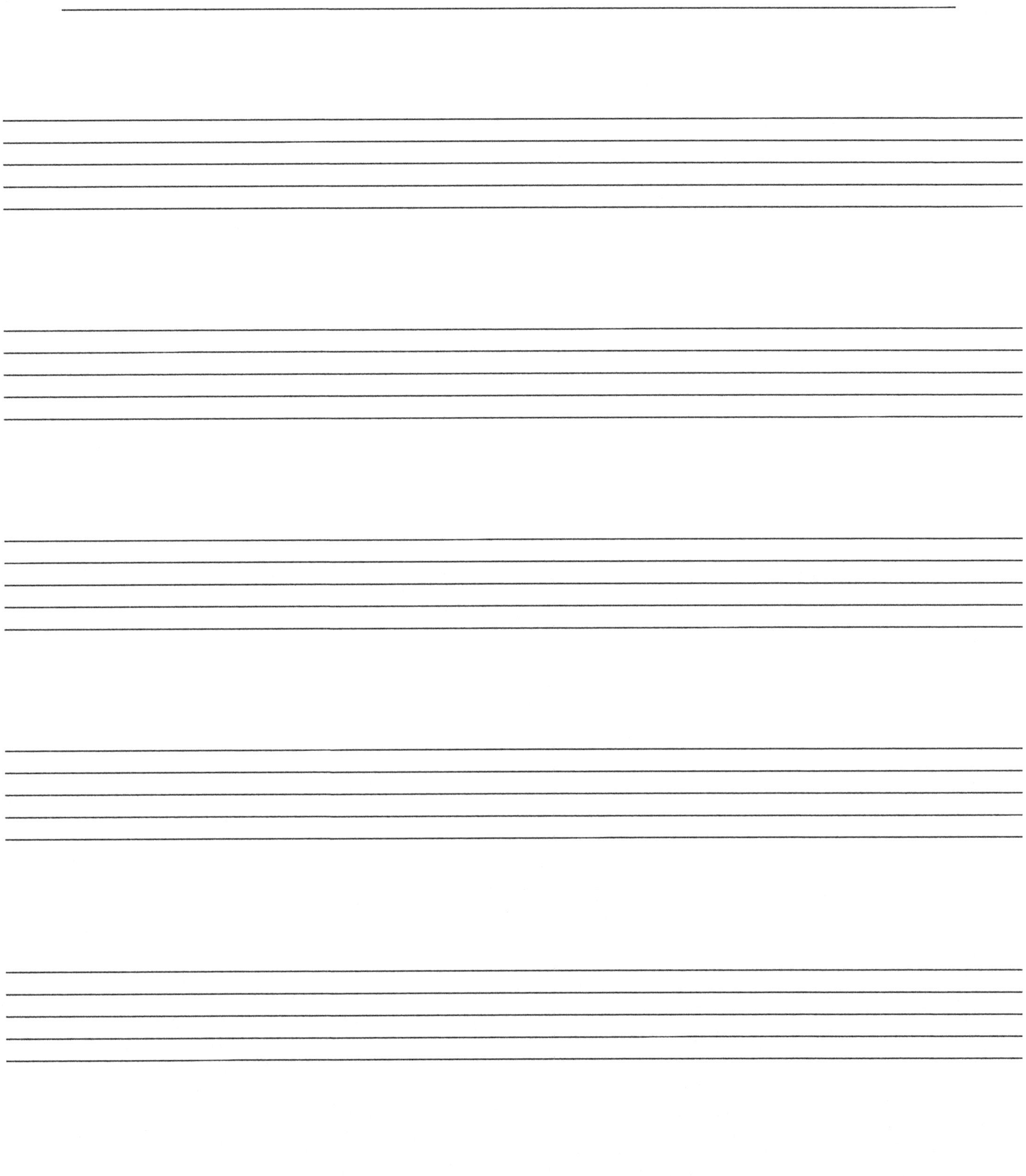

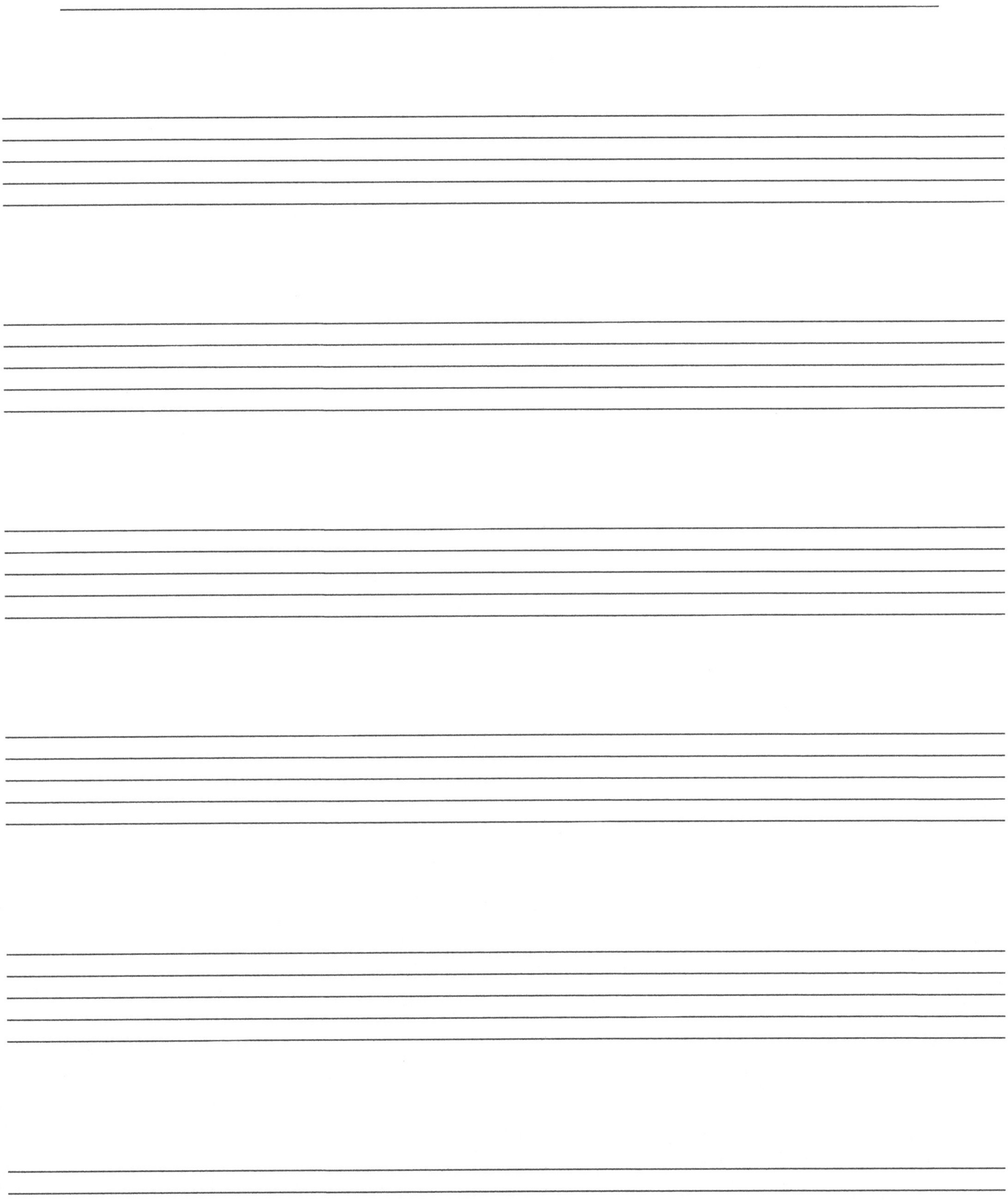

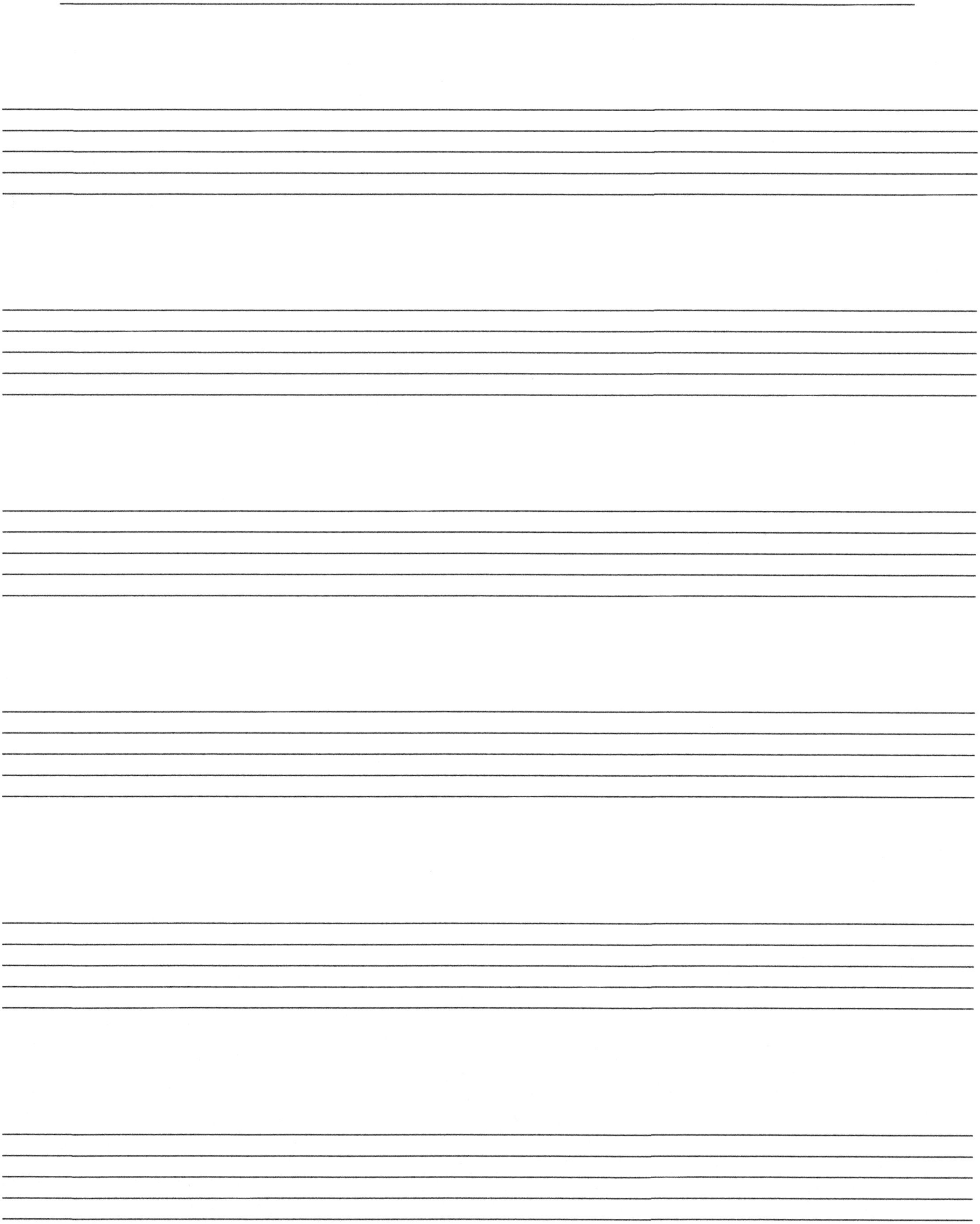

Made in the USA
Las Vegas, NV
28 July 2022

52309380R00057